THE MAN
WHO BECAME
A SCHOOL

Marcia S. Popp

ScarecrowEducation
Lanham, Maryland • Toronto • Oxford
2004

Published in the United States of America
by ScarecrowEducation
An imprint of The Rowman & Littlefield Publishing Group, Inc.
4501 Forbes Boulevard, Suite 200, Lanham, Maryland 20706
www.scarecroweducation.com

PO Box 317
Oxford
OX2 9RU, UK

British Library Cataloguing in Publication Information Available

Library of Congress Cataloging-in-Publication Data

Popp, Marcia S.
  The man who became a school / Marcia S. Popp.
    p. cm.
  Includes bibliographical references.
  ISBN 1-57886-152-7 (pbk. : alk. paper)
  1. Kamm, Charles. 2. Summerfield Grade School (Summerfield, Ill.) 3.
Teachers—Illinois—Summerfield—Biography. 4. School
principals—Illinois—Summerfield—Biography. I. Title.
LA2317.K25A3 2004
370'.92—dc22

                                                           2004003435

CONTENTS

CONTENTS

PRINCIPLES
OF THE PRINCIPAL

- Be a teacher first, regardless of your administrative title.
- Discover and encourage individual students' interests and capabilities.
- Nurture students as individuals.
- Value and support the individual temperaments and talents of teachers.
- Share what you know. Share what you are. Solve problems together.
- Pay attention to children. Listen to them; hear more than they say.
- Read good literature aloud to all grade levels.
- Give everyone a chance to show you their best selves.
- Provide support of the appropriate kind to everyone in the school family.
- Model respect for all work that serves others.
- Take children to places of lifelong learning and enjoyment.
- Involve the community in all activities of the school. Cultivate the media.
- Celebrate everyday and momentous occasions as a school family.
- Share leadership, so that others can learn to lead.

Drawn from the practice of Charles Kamm, principal and teacher at Summerfield Grade School, 1955–1993.

PREFACE

This is the story of Summerfield Grade School and Charles Kamm, a principal and teacher who devoted his entire professional career to this school. A modest man of quiet dignity, understated intelligence, wit and gracious manner, Mr. Kamm communicated his principles and sense of purpose to those around him for 38 years. He created a school family where each person was valued, and he encouraged the development of a community family where parents, grandparents, and citizens participated in the programs and activities of the school.

This book is not intended to be a nostalgic walk down memory lane, but rather an illustration of what is possible, when certain principles guide administrative decision making. Although Mr. Kamm's career as a teacher and principal came to a close in the 1990s, the basic principles of thought and behavior that directed his practice are timeless in their application. Schools, teachers, communities, and legal mandates change, but the core ideals of successful human relationships remain the same.

The general principles that guided Mr. Kamm's work with Summerfield Grade School are drawn from the panorama of his teaching and administrative performances and are illustrated with anecdotes, which demonstrate their application. As much as possible, I have used Mr. Kamm's own words, both from taped interviews and from our many informal conversations, to describe his beliefs about teaching and administration.

I have also relied on first-person accounts of students, faculty, parents, and community members who describe the influence Mr. Kamm had on individual children's lives—turning them around, making them into scholars, giving them hope, energizing or calming—as the occasion demanded.

Following each anecdotal chapter are sections titled "From Principles to Practice" and "To Consider." These provide opportunities for readers to reflect on the successful practice of one man and to examine themselves as educators in light of the challenges that face school leaders. Appendix A traces the history of principal-teachers, outlines current research related to the nurturing principal, and describes the legacy left to Summerfield School by Mr. Kamm. Appendix B contains a brief biography.

Why should you read this book? If you are considering teaching as a profession, or are planning to become a school administrator, this book will encourage you to examine your particular talents and use them to build a school family. If you are a parent, a school board member, or a citizen who takes an active interest in the quality of education in your community, you will discover new ways to support good teaching and competent educational leadership.

If you choose teaching for a career, you tread on hallowed ground. If you remain in the field, you will be a major influence in the lives of 20–80 children a year. If you move to a position of administrative authority, these numbers become exponential.

The kinds of people who spend so much time with the most precious of our national resources must be the few, the strong, the patient, the persistent, the most intelligent, and fiercely caring among us. And those who support these ideals and provide the resources and moral support to realize them must be the most intelligent, caring, and skilled persons that we can discover and recruit to the administration of education. This is a narrative account of one such man. I am honored that he consented to let me tell his story.

1

ON LOOKING
GLASS STREET

*If we work upon marble, it will perish; if we work upon brass, time
will efface it; if we rear temples, they will crumble into dust; but if
we work upon immortal minds, if we imbue them with principles,
with the just fear of God and love of our fellow-men, we engrave on
those tablets something which will brighten to all eternity.*

—Daniel Webster (2001, p. 481)

The Man Who Became a School is the story of one man whose career as a
principal and teacher contains a broad outline of principles that educational research has determined to be critical to the success of a principal's
work (Covey, 1991). Not everyone aspires to the administration of a rural
school, nor might they wish to remain in one small school for their entire career. But one man did, and although his story is not typical, it is instructive.

In his administration of Summerfield School, Charles Kamm exemplified
behaviors and attitudes that are characteristic of effective principals (Blase &
Kirby, 1999, p. 120). He was honest and selective in his praise, so that his
comments meant something to his teachers. Problems with instruction or
discipline were always discussed in private. He had high expectations for
both his students and teachers, and a strong belief in their abilities to succeed. Teachers were involved in decisions about instructional practices and
were encouraged to be creative and autonomous in their teaching.

Mr. Kamm believed that it was vital for teachers to have the materials and training necessary for instruction, and he worked tirelessly to provide them. He took an active interest in any discipline problems presented to teachers in the classroom and worked together with them to resolve difficulties with students or parents. At the same time, he often suggested alternative methods of handling these difficulties, sharing information helpful for understanding a child or instructional ideas that might modify behavior problems.

Mr. Kamm was his faculty's greatest champion in the larger arena of the school district, working to gain space, optimal class sizes, and instructional autonomy for his teachers. Because he was also a teacher, Mr. Kamm was able to model effective practice in his own classroom. All of his interactions reflected his belief in his teachers, his students, and his own teaching.

Researchers have discovered that the most effective principals are honest, highly visible, optimistic, and considerate (Blase & Kirby, 1999). Mr. Kamm demonstrated these qualities of character in an intense and consistent fashion. The Summerfield teachers were, in turn, talented, courageous, bold, flexible, funny, and loving persons. They stayed at Summerfield because they cared deeply about their students and the principal valued their work.

This account of Mr. Kamm's role as the principal/teacher of a small rural school will focus primarily on what he did to set a context for students and faculty to be their best selves. It should not be inferred, however, that every school day was blissful, or free from the distresses that plague every school. Teachers disagreed with one another, students misbehaved, parents complained, and higher levels of administration and school boards made unreasonable demands and uninformed decisions. Consolidation and redistricting played havoc with the functioning of an already successful school.

As in most school districts, there were children who presented particularly difficult challenges. Summerfield Grade School had its share of students from families who were on welfare or transient. While many came from middle-class and professional homes, others came to school hungry, tired, dirty, sick, poorly clothed, and physically or emotionally abused.

But, as Mr. Kamm was quick to point out, each child brought strengths to the school, either in terms of their individual temperaments and talents or their family backgrounds. Those from economically distressed homes frequently displayed an admirable resilience to poverty and had a fierce desire to achieve. Students from stable farm families brought a sturdy work ethic to school. Children of military personnel had a wealth of experiences to share from the wider world.

It was not paradise on Looking Glass Street in Summerfield, Illinois, but Summerfield Grade School was certainly a working family—one that took everyone in, encouraged them to achieve in ways they'd not thought possible, and cherished them, as only a family can.

The following chapters contain anecdotes that illustrate Mr. Kamm's teaching and administrative practices. Although they are told in story form, each was drawn from firsthand observation, either by the author or persons who worked closely with Mr. Kamm at the school—faculty, students, parents, and community members. These stories do more than illustrate one man's educational leadership. They provide a real-life illustration of what it means to nurture a school. And although Mr. Kamm's experiences took place in a small rural school, the general principles that directed his practice can be applied in other situations.

At any time during Charles Kamm's tenure as principal of Summerfield Grade School, visitors would be unlikely to find him in his office. If it was recess time, he would be on the playground, usually right in the middle of the action—pushing a merry-go-round full of kindergarten children or playing softball with the sixth graders. When teachers approached him for a quick conference, he still kept an eye on things—noticing if a child was courting an accident by swinging too high or watching a possible conflict in the making on the basketball court.

If a student stood on the sidelines, Mr. Kamm would strike up a casual conversation, commenting on the weather, inquiring about the individual child's interests, or encouraging him or her to join a game in progress.

Behind all the active participation and verbal interaction, there were distinct purposes. Mr. Kamm twirled the kindergarten children around on the merry-go-round because he truly enjoyed playing with them, but he also counted by ones, twos, fives, and tens as he pushed them, encouraging them to count along. Playing softball with his students provided him with information about how children related to one another and allowed him to recognize athletic ability in those who experienced academic difficulties.

Alert to situations that might result in accidents or precipitate fights, he headed off problems before they started, encouraging safety or urging students to use words instead of fists to settle differences. Noticing children who withdrew gave him the opportunity to provide encouragement and show interest in a child who felt isolated.

Mr. Kamm knew the boys who did not have fathers in the home and gave them extra attention. If a child came from an abusive home or one where grief had visited, he and his teachers made certain that the time spent at school was as happy as possible.

"Life doesn't always deal children a fair hand," he says. "We tried to create a place of stability, where they could be free from adult concerns for a least part of a day."

FROM PRINCIPLES TO PRACTICE

Mr. Kamm was able to provide encouragement, direction, and support to his school family because he had a realistic sense of his own strengths and a willingness to use them on behalf of the welfare of others. He believed that a principal should be the principal *teacher*, learning and sharing as much as possible. He enjoyed teaching and transformed the simplest of activities into an occasion for learning. Each child was valued, and no one was lost in the shuffle. There was a constant drawing in from the sidelines, where children in grief tend to cluster. Mr. Kamm was alert to situations that might make a painful day more bearable for his students. By showing genuine interest in them and paying attention to what they had to say, Mr. Kamm encouraged the development of self-worth in his students.

TO CONSIDER

What kind of school did you attend as a child? Was it large, small, rural, or urban? Did you enjoy school? What was your experience with the principal? How would you set up lines of communication with your faculty that would allow you to relate to your students as individuals? If you were to lead a large school, how would you get to know as many students as possible? How important do you think it is for the principal to relate to students as individuals? What strengths of character and intelligence would you bring to a school family?

2

A CALM,
KAMM PRESENCE

*There was a child went forth every day; and the first object he
look'd upon, that object he became; and that object became part of
him for the day, or a certain part of the day; or for many years, or
stretching cycles of years.*

—Walt Whitman (1996, p. 3)

Charles Kamm used to say that most of what he learned about teaching
was an accident. A more accurate description might be "incidental."
His intuitions were good, and he learned quickly how to recognize potential
learning opportunities and capitalize on them.

When clover began to cover the school lawn in the spring, students were
encouraged to be the first one to find one with four leaves. Why did it have
four leaves? What else did they find on the ground when they were down
there on their hands and knees? Mr. Kamm believed that children learned
naturally, by observing their environment and the people in it; their innate
curiosity could be used to teach concepts from any discipline.

In the classroom, Mr. Kamm's teaching style was traditional—the very
best of that genre. His manner engaged students, and the unpredictability of
the way he called on students kept them on the edge of their seats. Mr. Kamm
was never dull. It was easy to see that he was passionate about learning and
demanded a student's best effort in class, from start to finish. He always

accepted children at their own level and worked tirelessly to help them elevate that level. No one got a pass. He expected everyone to learn and made that very clear.

Observers in Mr. Kamm's fifth-grade classroom witnessed multidimensional lessons, consisting of the topic at hand, meanings of words, spelling, grammar, math, science, history, literature, and puns. The various elements of instruction danced separately and together in a ballet of extraordinary teaching.

Woven into the academics was also an emphasis on manners—the polite way to address the teacher and other students; the considerate way to disagree; and possible ways to show appreciation for others' contributions. He gave reasons for the manners he expected. If students dawdled in the hallway at break time, he reminded them that it was a courtesy to the teacher and other students not to delay instruction.

Mr. Kamm held his students' constant attention by involving them with questions, asking their opinions—noting ideas, metaphors, and interesting words. Any reading aloud was an occasion to learn new words or to notice the beauty of certain phrases or descriptions. The world map was always pulled down and dictionaries were at hand for students to look up new words or quickly locate cities, countries, and continents mentioned during instruction. Questions that could not be immediately answered were listed on the board for later research by students and teacher.

In Mr. Kamm's English classes, students analyzed grammatical structures and searched for new words to express their ideas. Correct spelling and grammar were drilled into his students so carefully and consistently that junior high and high school English teachers were able to identify his students by their proficiency in these areas.

Mr. Kamm was at school early in the morning, inspecting the physical plant and noticing anything that might need repair or maintenance. As teachers arrived, he went from room to room to greet them, asking about their families, inquiring if there was anything he could do to help with student problems, offering to read aloud or do a science experiment with the class.

He was at the curb when the school buses arrived, meeting the children before they entered the school, calming them from the boisterous bus ride. He was in the hall, greeting students as they passed him by. After recess, he sat in the middle of the hall, grading papers. They passed him quietly. His presence was enough to inspire order.

Mr. Kamm recognized the individual and collective worth of students and staff and sought ways to share that recognition. He knew each classroom as if it were his own, and all children as if they were his own students. He frequently and sincerely noticed and commended the efforts of teachers, and discretely assisted those who were struggling.

Others might not have worked so hard with every student, knowing that many would not attend college or enter professions. But the same quality of study was required of every child. It was important to Mr. Kamm that future truck drivers as well as future lawyers know something about the good, the true, and the beautiful. He taught to children's souls, showing them what there was to enjoy in classical music and artistic masterpieces. By reading aloud from the classics, he exposed students to the finest and most lyrical examples of prose and poetry.

Letters of appreciation from students, parents, faculty, and community members echo a common theme: Mr. Kamm's beliefs about people and their potential created a school community that was uncommon in its caring and ambition for each child. He was enthusiastic in his teaching, and it was contagious. He cared deeply, and it showed in children's memories, even after they had become adults. His firm and fair attitude was a model for them, and his tireless sense of humor reassured students and faculty alike. He was a calm presence and an exciting force that provided both stability and stimulus to the school.

Mr. Kamm did not become a teacher because he thought he could do nothing else. He taught every level of elementary school, either as the assigned teacher, adjunct instructor in a particular subject, or substitute teacher. He enjoyed teaching students of every age.

As a teacher, principal, or superintendent, Mr. Kamm was not consumed with numbers, statistics, projections, and positioning himself for bonuses, raises, and promotion. This disengagement gave him the freedom to pursue other goals, such as making certain that every child felt like a special person, that every child was successful at something—anything; that every faculty member felt supported in their teaching.

When Mr. Kamm was appointed principal of Summerfield Grade School, he refused to continue as an administrator unless he could also teach part time. Few people knew, nor did he divulge this information himself, that he turned down a raise so that a younger teacher could remain on the payroll.

"He had a family and needed the money," he said, when asked about the episode. "I didn't have a family yet," he explained simply, "and he was a good teacher."

FROM PRINCIPLES TO PRACTICE

Mr. Kamm enjoyed working with students of all ages and appreciated the unique personality and potential of each child in his care. He chose teaching as a career because he believed that he had something of value to share with students and a school family. Everyone was valued, each had potential, and Mr. Kamm was the first to notice and encourage growth and achievement. For him, the role of principal was a person to be, rather than a list of things to do.

TO CONSIDER

How important would it be for you to continue teaching as part of your assignment as a principal? What academic area is of special interest to you? In what ways might you share this interest with the students in your school, in your role as principal? In what ways might this interest or ability be shared with your faculty? How will you demonstrate your own enthusiasm for learning to the students in your school? In what ways might you indicate your concern for the problems of individual students and faculty? How important to a student's learning is the context in which he learns?

3

READ THE
LAST PAGE FIRST

Once at a revival meeting, I heard a preacher say, "Faith is when you hear the bird singing before the egg is hatched." Teachers have that kind of faith in their pupils or they would not be able to teach. They see promise, sometimes when no one else can see it, and over and over, because of their faith, they work hard enough to make the promise come true.

—Jean Little (1991, p. 57)

Watching Charles Kamm at work was like trying to keep track of every-thing going on in a three-ring circus. There were many levels in the things he said and did, and none of them were trivial. A lover of words, he did not miss an occasion to create puns, as much to amuse himself as anyone else. Indeed, many were so subtle that they could only be discovered from verbatim notes that recorded his teaching or interactions with students, parents, and teachers.

Audio-recording and even videotaping these events could not capture the range of interaction beyond the tape recorder's or camera's range. Writing down everything he said involved looking, listening, and recording, all at the same time. His gestures, tone, and manner were as much a part of what he said, as were the words.

Mr. Kamm had great faith in the potential of his students and faculty. One of his habits, when he picked up a book to read to students, was to read the last page. If he liked what he read, he would read the book. If the book didn't come out right, he didn't want to bother with it. There had to be something worthy about the words and story for him to share it with others.

He always looked to the ultimate value of an activity or decision by considering what its final results might be. The last page was always the bottom line for him. If something might help a child gain self-confidence, become more sensitive to beauty in nature or the arts, help them become more compassionate or understanding of those around them, then this justified whatever activity would best bring this about.

If Mr. Kamm had based his work with children on the first page of their school lives with him, he might not have invested so much attention and care in them, because many seemed either hopeless, hapless, or both. But he looked beyond first impressions, saw each child as a person with limitless potential, and made the last page of the book come true, for as many children as possible. Like the principal quoted from Jean Little's book in the chapter epigraph, he listened for—and heard—the singing.

When Mr. Kamm was a young student, he was described in teachers' comments on report cards and by his former science teacher as someone who could be serious, but witty; calm, but passionate about things he believed in. He was "no nonsense," one teacher wrote, "but funny—clever in word play and puns."

Others noticed that he was a calm young man, but exceptionally alert to people in his environment, often knowing them much better than might be imagined. He was described as intelligent, but not showy; happy and content, but fiery about injustices.

Years later, these same traits of personality and character lent themselves to the education of children. He learned and grew and tried new things, but the essential ways that he taught and interacted with people remained the same. He was polite, but straightforward—kind, but firm. His discipline was strict, but always fair. He was flexible in his response to situations, but constant in his moral outlook.

Teachers described him as consistent in the behavior he expected, but that he treated each person as an individual. They characterized him as both quiet and fun, serious, and witty. He was all business, one teacher observed, but loved surprises and spontaneous lessons. Throughout his life, Charles Kamm has been a man of great consistency in his contradictions.

In *Where Are You From?* (Loehring, 1989), a story of growing up in Summerfield written by one of Mr. Kamm's former students, the author describes Mr. Kamm as "the kind of teacher I would eventually aspire to be—funny, interesting, challenging and articulate" (p. 74).

Wayne Loehring, who later became a history teacher and coach, describes Mr. Kamm from a student's point of view:

> He was a disciplinarian, impeccably honest and forthright. He loved his students, and it showed. He put in extra hours, never missed a day of work and enjoyed teaching. For the first time in my short career as an elementary student, I had a male teacher to follow and emulate. . . .
>
> Mr. Kamm devoted one Saturday night every month to chaperoning roller skating parties for students. As a result, school became important to me, but at the time, I didn't realized how it would influence my life, or just how Mr. Kamm's teaching affected me. . . .
>
> I vividly recall my seventh and eighth grade years. There were normal happenings: school dances, basketball games, field trips, and of course, homework. . . . I remember diagramming sentence after sentence on the chalkboard and labeling every part of speech. After that, English was never difficult for me in high school or college, because writing and using good grammar was easy. I also remember completing my first research paper, coupling research with writing skills. I wrote my paper on the Civil War and became a Civil War buff as a result. (Loehring, 1989, pp. 74–78)

Christine Lanning, coteacher with Mr. Kamm in fifth grade, had also been his student when she was a fifth grader. "It was always my dream, as a child, to grow up and teach at Summerfield School," she says. "Mr. Kamm told us there was a shortage of teachers, and he was the reason I went into teaching."

Mr. Kamm was a friend of Christine's family and often took her and her brothers fishing and mushroom hunting in the summer. "On Saturdays, he took us to the zoo and we'd have a picnic in Forest Park," she says.

She also remembers the field trips they took in school. "Mr. Kamm would say 'Bring your gym shoes tomorrow. We're going on a nature walk.' My grandfather was the school janitor at that time," Christine says. "He would go ahead and start a fire for us, and we would roast wieners after our hike."

"I still take my class on nature walks," she adds. "I do it because he did, and I remember how much fun it was. I also love history, because he made it fun. When he taught anything, he made it come alive."

A close reading of Mr. Kamm's correspondence through the years reveals someone who continued to take an active interest in his students' lives. There were many thank you notes for letters of recommendation, letters telling of achievements, or disappointments. Others simply wanted him to know how much his faith in them had meant, not only at the time, but as a continuing force in their lives. Recently he received this note:

Hi, Mr. Kamm:

I stopped by your house on November 4th and left a note on your chalkboard. I was your student in 8th grade at Summerfield in 1969–1970. I am writing to thank you for all you did for me and Jon, my brother, and for your kindness to Sarah, my mother, when we moved to Summerfield.

I have been a lawyer for 20 years now, and file air pollution and water pollution lawsuits for the state of Missouri. I still have the longhand report I wrote for you on Earth Day about water pollution. I bet neither of us ever guessed in 1970, that the report would turn into a career.

Jon lives outside Chicago. He has an engineering degree from the University of Illinois and an MBA from DePaul University in Chicago. You were a great teacher and a good friend. Thank you. Robert and Jon Cook really appreciated you and still remember you.

Grace and peace,
Robert Cook
(Assistant Attorney General for the State of Missouri)

It became clear, from these, and other unsolicited communications, that Mr. Kamm's beliefs about people and their potential had made a significant difference in the way students viewed the world and directed their careers.

Perhaps the most important thing Mr. Kamm did as principal, however, was to create a family of the entire community, of which the school was an important member. His faculty and students regarded him as the father of the school, and most of them have stayed close to this family.

A token of the esteem in which he is held is the fact that almost everyone addresses him as "Mr. Kamm" (including the author). Family members and a few others call him "Charles," but he would never be called "Charlie," except in fun, the year his teachers made T-shirts emblazoned with "Charlie's Angels," to celebrate his 25th year of teaching.

Like all successful educators, he shared his interests with his students. More than that, he shared his enthusiasm for these interests and anything connected to learning about new things—music, art, literature, or nature. He saw the position of principal as an opportunity to bring children experiences they might otherwise not have.

Mr. Kamm's belief in his students echoed the belief of Jesse Stuart (1958): "In any youth who has ever come to school to me, I have seen something essentially good, a potential that needs to be developed. It is the teacher's duty to develop this good potential in each young individual" (p. 7).

When asked about teachers who influenced him, Mr. Kamm described them as firm, competent, and businesslike—qualities that would also define his own teaching. One of his teachers was Suzanne Wicks, retired and in her 90s, still living and active in the community. In a phone interview, Mrs. Wicks described her experience with Mr. Kamm when he was a young high school student (personal communication, 2002).

Suzanne Wicks taught independent study and honors classes in science at Lebanon High School. These classes were college-level instruction, and she had students study fossils, which were everywhere in the area. She tried to find a student's interest and forward their understanding of it—from ornithology to biochemistry, in which she earned a Ph.D. at the age of 70.

Mrs. Wicks was an innovative teacher, especially for her time. She trained promising students as lab assistants, giving them responsibilities for setting up equipment and providing instructional support to their classmates. Their work paralleled that of university lab assistants, and in return for their diligence, each was privileged to wear a white lab coat, procured from nearby Scott Air Force Base. She incorporated student team teaching into her classes, and encouraged students to help one another with explanations of course material.

Her enthusiasm must have been contagious. She reports getting up every morning, eager to see how plants in the lab were growing. She couldn't wait to get to school, and often found students already at the door. It is easy to see why Mr. Kamm would name her as influential in his life, because his own innovative teaching and enthusiasm for learning mirrored that of his high school mentor.

Mrs. Wicks described Mr. Kamm as a slight, serious young boy, who quickly completed homework in study hall and was prone to talking or entertaining fellow students with the extra time on his hands. He was also bored in many classes, so she asked to have him placed in her advanced physics class, where he excelled.

She also approached the president of historic McKendree College in Lebanon and asked if he could attend summer school. At 15, the young boy was required to take the regular entrance exam and achieved a perfect score. Thereafter, he took college classes in the summer and by the time he graduated from high school, he was able to enter college as a sophomore. He graduated from McKendree in 3 years with majors in history and German.

Mr. Kamm's teaching reflected many of his own early experiences in school. No student was bored because he challenged them with every sentence to discover more about a topic, or the words used to describe it. He was also careful with his noticing, observing those who might need extra help, encouragement, or concerned attention.

Mr. Kamm's two sons attended Summerfield School, and he taught them both. They were excellent students, and when asked if it was difficult not to show favoritism, he replied, "Chuck said I never called on him when he raised his hand. But he was smart and quick and always had his hand up. He got the same attention as all the others."

Teachers and former students believe that having his sons in his class worked, because Mr. Kamm was perceived as the father of all the students. He is remembered by teachers and students alike as being extremely fair. He noticed them all, talked to them, and played with them. While his boys were at school, they were part of a family of 120 other children.

FROM PRINCIPLES TO PRACTICE

Mr. Kamm saw potential in every child sent to him, even when they were showing him their worst. He withheld judgment, even when a situation seemed obvious. Throughout his career, he modeled an enthusiasm and excitement for learning, sharing his talents and interests with the entire school. In the process, he created a family—one that would continually "listen for the singing."

TO CONSIDER

Which teachers inspired you when you were a student in elementary or high school? Can you identify their influence in your own teaching or in the way you aspire to teach? Did you ever attend a school where the principal was also a teacher? How might a principal assume a teaching role, even if this were not part of an administrative assignment?

4

BEES MADE THIS?

All of my life before and my life after is justified by the wonder of this moment.

—Sylvia Ashton-Warner (1986, p. 200)

Through the years, Mr. Kamm was honored on various occasions for the achievements of Summerfield Grade School. He found it difficult to accept any credit that was singled out to him, saying that "what was good at Summerfield Grade School was mostly a 'we,' not an 'I' thing."

He was proud of his teachers and an enthusiastic host to community members, parents, preservice teachers, and college faculty. Students in the teacher education program at nearby McKendree College were frequent visitors, observers, and participants in the activities at Summerfield. They enjoyed working with students of all ages—reading aloud, helping with projects, and observing master teachers at work.

They joined Summerfield students, faculty, staff (and principal) in their all-school, silent, sustained reading periods, and watched as older and younger classes matched up to read to each other in the "Book Buddies" program.

Teacher education classes enthusiastically applauded Mrs. Nave's kindergarten play adaptation of *Tikki, Tikki, Tembo* (Mosel, 1989) and observed Kay Dunn, the primary Title I specialist, as she worked patiently with children to help build their skills in reading and math.

They watched Becky Culler write out words that individual first graders wanted to learn to read, and saw her students measure everything in their room, as part of a math activity.

In later years, the McKendree students watched Chrissie Cook introduce a weekly theme—bears, penguins, historical figures—where language arts, science, history, geography, music, art, and math became tools to study favorite topics. Every week, first graders learned to read a new poem and song, prepared a food, created a drama, and participated in math activities related to them. Mrs. Cook brought in tubs full of books from the library in nearby Mascoutah—books for students to read and books to read aloud.

Interested in new ways to set up a classroom, the teachers-in-training explored the learning stations in Pat Sheahan's second-grade classroom. They read the students' letters to popular children's authors and were delighted when the class received responses from Tomi de Paola, Robert Munsch, Patricia Palucco, and Jan Brett.

In Ingrid Owen's third-grade classroom, they noticed how art had been integrated into the curriculum, and saw students holding tiny images of the *Indian in the Cupboard* (Banks, 1999), as they listened to Mrs. Owens read the book aloud to the class. They read books that her children had written and illustrated as part of the "Young Authors" program.

They saw fourth-grade students in Julia Parker's room learn to appreciate Michelangelo's work on the ceiling of the Sistine Chapel by lying on their backs to draw on paper taped to the bottom of their desks. They also watched with considerable interest as children carefully dissected fumigated owl pellets, and listened to them exclaim over what they found inside.

They observed Christine Lanning's patient and reassuring manner with her students, and watched as her fifth graders presented an exhibition of Indian culture to the entire school. Later in the week, McKendree visitors read about the demonstration in the local newspaper, which showed the students grinding corn and making Indian arrowheads from flint rock.

They watched Jim Furtkamp play softball on the playground with his sixth-grade class, and then calm them down after recess by reading to them from *Maniac Magee* (Spinelli, 2000). They noticed the students' delight when they came into the classroom one morning and saw that Deb Cryder, the Title I teacher, had created Maniac Magee's ball of string, and hung it from the back blackboard.

On one occasion, the science teaching methods class from McKendree was invited to join Mrs. Nave's kindergarten for a celebration of insects. Students had added a word about insects to their key words every day for the preceding two weeks. Sentences on the storyboard included "Insects have six legs," "Spiders are not insects," and "There are three parts to an insect."

As part of the insect celebration, Mrs. Nave showed the class a honeycomb and asked the children if they knew what it was. She wrote down their guesses, and then asked them if they would like to taste a little of the syrup that had run out of the comb. Each dabbed a finger in the sweet stickiness and almost immediately, one child exclaimed "Honey!"

"What *is* that thing the honey is in?" one asked, impatiently.

Mrs. Nave nodded at one of the McKendree students, who told the class that it was a honeycomb, and that the bees had made it themselves.

"Oooh," the children said in a chorus, and at once there was a babble of discussion about how a bee could do such a thing.

Mrs. Nave regularly brought in fruits and vegetables for children to sample on tasting day—asparagus, mangos, okra, seedless grapes, bean sprouts, avocados, and black cherries. For many of the children in her class, these foods were as foreign to them as couscous or sushi might be to other children of this age.

Each teacher helped polish a dimension of a child's total schooling at Summerfield and Mr. Kamm respected and cherished the diverse talents each faculty member contributed to students' learning. When teachers were successful, he was happy for them, and let them know it. When there were disappointments, he comforted and encouraged them. When there were difficulties, he saw any problem as *theirs* to solve together.

In a newspaper article, Mrs. Nave once wrote, "It was not necessary for him to be a despot to succeed as a principal. Although Mr. Kamm is characterized as caring, supportive and kind, he could also grab the reins and do or say what had to be done or said, when the occasion called for it" (Nave, 1981, p. 1).

"He had the ability," one parent said, "to slice crisply to the point and say precisely what needed to be said." And then the caveat heard so many times over the years—"but he was never hurtful."

Only Mr. Kamm and those close to the Summerfield teachers knew how much extra time they all spent to provide special experiences for their students, or how much of their own money they used to purchase materials and books for children to enjoy. Only a few knew how the seventh- and eighth-grade basketball team got their uniforms.

The faculty at Summerfield was a group of distinct individuals, and each brought to his or her own teaching a wide range of talents and methodologies. But they were united in their belief that they could make a difference in their students' lives. Some were strict, others were more lenient, in terms of what they considered acceptable classroom behavior. But each was determined to be fair and all tried their best to be honest and direct with their students.

Because the principal and faculty lived in close proximity to their student population, they knew the expectations of parents, the types of discipline used in various homes, and the hopes of each family for their children. They also knew who didn't get breakfast in the morning, who hadn't changed clothes in a week, who showed up with unexplained bruises, and whose family could not afford school supplies.

The Summerfield teachers were resourceful in their efforts to obtain funds for school activities. Classrooms sponsored a variety of fundraisers, from selling candy to bake sales. These monies were then put into a common fund, which bought supplies for art projects, books for the library, and software for the computers. When a particular classroom had a specific pressing need, the money was relegated by turns into places where it would do the most good.

Asked what he did when teachers experienced difficulties with a particular child, Mr. Kamm replied: "First I'd drop in and see what was happening. I'd also make a point of talking to the child, to see what else was going on in their lives. With any child that presented a problem to a teacher, I made it *our* problem and we worked on it together."

Sometimes, it came down to how a child presented himself. A student might come to school dirty, hungry, tired, frightened, or suspicious of adults. Bravado often stood in for fear of failure. For these children, Mr. Kamm reminded the teachers that "anybody can love the easy kids—the ones who are clean, bright, say all the right things and behave themselves. It takes real effort to work with the difficult ones."

"Try loving them," he suggested. It was advice he modeled in his own teaching.

Helping a child wash up in the restroom, getting food from the cafeteria, and providing clothes, shoes, or a coat as needed gave deprived students a greater chance of paying attention and gaining acceptance from their peers. No child was ever excluded from an activity or outing because of a lack of ability to pay. The principal and teachers always had extra admission monies and spare lunches on hand, which were distributed discretely to those who needed them.

Patience and extra attention from both the teacher and the principal often worked magic on children who acted out, sometimes in response to verbal or physical abuse outside of school. When boys did not have a father in their homes, Mr. Kamm invited them to his office to share a book or talk about problems they were having.

"A fishing trip, mushroom hunt, or arrowhead expedition provided additional informal times to talk things over, or just provide quiet, accepting companionship," he says.

Students attending Summerfield Grade School came in all shapes and sizes, from different racial backgrounds, caring homes and those that were abusive. Some came from homes of privilege and others barely subsisted at the poverty level. Often, children were moved around from school to school, and academic performance suffered. The faculty at Summerfield worked successfully with all of these children. Each approached teaching in a different manner, but all were effective in helping students learn and grow. In their individual ways, Summerfield teachers and their principal cherished every child put in their care.

This variety of teaching approaches was critical for teachers in training to observe. The semester that a student spends as an apprentice teacher is one of the most important experiences in teacher education. This is the time and place where mentor relationships are formed, models for teaching are internalized, and habits of practice are established. Every student needs just the right teacher to make the transition from being a student to leading classroom instruction.

Summerfield was the first, and most consistently cooperative, school to allow instructors from McKendree to observe in their classrooms for the purpose of placing student teachers. It was always a joint venture, beginning with: "I have this student who needs help with classroom management. Do you think you could help her?" or "This is a student who has observed you, and wants to learn more about how you put a program together. Would you accept him?"

Many schools in the area did not allow college instructors to visit classes or make suggestions about placement with specific teachers. The practice of placing student observers or student teachers in classrooms by random procedures rarely worked out as well as those who were carefully planned in advance. Supervising teachers did not have to be perfect, but ideally, they were enthusiastic about their teaching, loved what they were doing, and were eager to share their ideas with others.

Of course placement mistakes were made, even with the best intentions by all concerned. But when this happened, the Summerfield teachers were forgiving. Any problem with a student teacher was a shared problem, and the situation was worked out in the best possible way. Mr. Kamm and his faculty believed in second chances, and in some cases, a third.

McKendree students were inspired to reach levels of achievement of which they did not know they were capable. Many repaid their supervising teachers by becoming exemplary teachers themselves, earning recognition at the state and national levels in states from Alaska to Florida.

This openness to visitors from the college provided a steady stream of new ideas to share with the McKendree students. Mr. Kamm and his teachers invited preservice teachers to visit on a regular basis, and entire methods classes were welcomed into the school to observe lessons and interact with children in the classroom. For 10 years, McKendree College had a lab school, where hundreds of students learned from master teachers, as observers, classroom participants, student teachers, and invited guests.

Mr. Kamm had deep respect for his teachers. He spoke proudly of the efforts of each to work with the wide range of abilities in their classrooms. Special programs, projects, and displays were pointed out and shared. It was evident that he trusted his teachers to give their best, and they didn't disappoint him.

Asked to describe his faculty, Mr. Kamm characterized each one in terms of the strengths they brought to their teaching and interaction with children. Terms of character, such as calm, steady, cheerful, pleasant, caring, patient, fair, and genuinely concerned, appeared frequently in these descriptions.

When he portrayed individual faculty members in terms of their teaching performance, he noted that they were knowledgeable about their subject matter, enthusiastic about teaching, and had high expectations for their students' learning—all characteristics shown by research to be related to student achievement (Phi Delta Kappa Workshop, 1972).

He further described his teachers as persons who consistently pursued excellence, challenged students, communicated well, adapted to changing conditions, were eager to learn, and were willing to try new approaches to teaching. To Mr. Kamm, his teachers were as unique in their talents and strengths as were the children they taught.

In the early 1990s, McKendree College received a 3-year grant from the Emerson Electric Company in St. Louis to improve reading instruction in a five-county region. At this time, the practice of using literature and the language arts as tools for learning all subjects in the curriculum was just beginning to influence classroom teaching in local school districts. Teachers were encouraged to teach reading by having children read real books. Literature circles, silent sustained reading, book buddies, and journaling were in their infant stages.

Summerfield already followed many of these practices, as most teachers integrated what they were studying in one content area with the others, as a matter of course. All teachers read aloud to their classes daily, and there was a successful cross-grade reading program in place.

With Mr. Kamm's support and encouragement, the teachers at Summerfield enrolled as a group in a course taught through McKendree College. Subsequently, they experimented with the new ideas in teaching reading and adapted them to their own teaching styles.

In a move that challenged administrative decisions at the district level, Mr. Kamm and his teachers requested permission to dismiss the purchase of basal readers and workbooks for the following year. Each teacher worked out their own curriculum for teaching reading, using classic children's literature and notebooks that helped students practice reading and writing skills. This was a gigantic leap of faith for teachers and a principal whose reputations were on the line to make this approach work.

At that time, Summerfield Grade School was the first school in Illinois to adopt an integrated language arts program (then called whole language) in all of their classrooms. Mr. Kamm and the Summerfield teachers were featured in two Emerson Electric reports, an interview on National Public Radio, and a presentation to the Lewis and Clark Reading Council, an affiliate of the International Reading Association. Mr. Kamm and the Summerfield faculty were also chronicled in the *St. Louis Commerce Magazine* in January 1992.

During the second year of the grant, Summerfield teachers invited other teachers from four neighboring counties to visit the school on a Saturday, where they talked about what they were doing and how they did it. Their modesty removed the threat and suspicion that sometimes attends teacher presentations to other teachers.

Even when complimented on their teaching, Summerfield teachers always replied that they didn't have all the answers. They saw themselves as lifelong learners who would forever be finding new ideas to make their teaching better. Visiting teachers toured the classrooms and picked up teaching tips and copies of books that would help them get started, if the new approach looked interesting.

The Summerfield teachers, modest about telling other teachers what they did in class, were nervous at first. But as visitors leaned forward to hear what they had to say, asked questions, and requested permission to visit them, they welcomed their new adult students with open arms and the excited concern of mentors.

One of the conditions for teachers to attend the Saturday sessions was an agreement from their respective school districts that they would be granted a professional day to visit their mentor's classroom during school hours to see these practices in action. Through these visits, friendships were forged, Summerfield teachers were asked to make presentations at other schools, and a circle of support began to form among teachers from all over the region.

Many of these friendships have lasted through the years, and the ideas shared with one another have extended into the teaching community at large—more widespread than might ever have been hoped, by a group of modest, but exceptionally talented teachers and their principal.

FROM PRINCIPLES TO PRACTICE

Mr. Kamm believed that a principal should not delegate responsibility, but rather share it. He knew his teachers well enough to appreciate their individual character strengths and teaching abilities. Each was valued for his or her unique talents, and was supported in his or her efforts to learn and grow as a professional. He embraced opportunities for his staff to explore new teaching methods, and championed their efforts to share ideas with teachers from other schools.

TO CONSIDER

What do you remember about your observation experiences or student teaching? What was the process of placement in the college or university where you attended? If you had a good experience, how might you help create the same situation for teachers-in-training in your school? If you had a negative experience, how might you help prevent this from happening in your school, through your intervention or leadership as a principal?

5

MISS ELSIE AND
THE FLAT TIRE

A teacher affects eternity; he can never tell where his influence stops.

—Henry Adams (1999, p. 300)

One of Mr. Kamm's defining principles was to "share what you are, and share what you've been given." He saw all the interests and skills that he'd developed in his lifetime as gifts to use as an educational leader.

"Some people give children things," he once commented. "I give them experiences."

As a young principal, he often worked with teachers older than himself. One of these was the first-grade teacher at Summerfield. He tells of a time when he was leaving school for the evening:

> I went out and found Miss Elsie trying to change a flat tire on her car. It was jacked up in a precarious manner, so I asked if I could help her. She said "yes," and gave me the keys to open the trunk to get the spare. It was completely flat.
>
> "Won't that do, Mr. Kamm?" she asked me.
>
> "I'm afraid not, Miss Elsie," I said, and we took the flat to be fixed.

Miss Elsie's experience with the flat tire became a metaphor for Mr. Kamm's interaction with parents, teachers, and students. Miss Elsie had never changed a tire, and had no idea what was involved. Mr. Kamm shared the expertise he had with her and did not judge her for not knowing how to do something she'd never done before.

Similarly, when students or faculty needed help, Mr. Kamm did not see them as ignorant, only as not informed or unskilled. He believed it was his business to provide that information or help them develop the requisite skill.

His deep respect for the ideas and interests of others is found in the way he embraced all aspects of community life. In his office and home, he played classical music. However, he was equally comfortable with the popular tunes of the bowling alley or the skating rink, where he joined his students for an evening's entertainment. His refined tastes in music and art were not something that separated him from his charges, but something to share.

He played softball with the students, walked around and observed their play, and frequently joined in. When rain, snow, or high winds curtailed outdoor recess, he made certain that everyone had a good time indoors. He organized basketball games, softball catch, and relays—appropriate to the ages of individual classes. Disappointment about not being able to play outdoors was soon dispelled, as children ran, played, and shouted, drowning out the sound of pounding rain on the gym roof and warming up the space that gave them a safe haven from wind or blowing snow.

Mr. Kamm learned early about promising rewards for academic performance. When he was a beginning teacher, he promised a dollar to every student who earned a hundred on a geography test. He was nearly broke by the end of the day. As with all such experiences, he says, "I learned something." What he learned helped him convince decades of students that learning was its own reward, and that the thrill of success far outran any monetary reward.

The use of proper grammar and the correct spelling of words in all subject areas was an important goal in Mr. Kamm's teaching. Prospective teachers were asked to write their philosophy of education before he approved their hiring.

"What the teachers didn't know," he says, "was that I was checking for good grammar and correct spelling, as much as their ideas about teaching." He believed firmly in the role of good models. If teachers were not able to meet the standards expected of students, they weren't hired.

A hometown boy, slight, shy, and precocious, Mr. Kamm might have grown up to be an astronaut, an Ivy League English professor, a geologist, research scientist, musician, artist, or foreign diplomat. He had the native ability and academic qualifications to seek a career in all of these prestigious and high-powered areas.

Instead, he chose to use his talents to interest generations of young people in science, literature, music, art, and the power of well-spoken words. He didn't blast off from Cape Canaveral, but every year, students from the entire school shared the excitement as fifth graders launched the rockets they had constructed under his supervision. He watched with delight as kindergarten children took turns racing after the rockets, to retrieve them when they fell to earth. Each waited eagerly for the day when they would launch their own.

Mr. Kamm didn't pursue a career in university teaching, but every student of his knew the value of correct grammar and proper spelling, and each heard the classics of literature read aloud in the classroom. His interests in geology, biology, and chemistry brought the classroom and surrounding area alive with rock collecting, mushroom hunting, and exciting laboratory demonstrations.

His proficiency in languages and diplomatic skills enhanced his teaching and enabled him to relate in exceptional and productive ways with a widely diverse school population and the broader community. A lifelong love of music and art prompted him to take the entire school to St. Louis each year, to experience live symphonic performances and displays at the art museum.

Mr. Kamm was the product of local schools and a local college. He chose to spend his career as the leader of a local school. He believed that his familiarity with the area and its people gave him a head start in educating its children. As a child, he had explored the area—its woods, creeks, fishing holes, and geological features. It was fun for him to share these special places with his students.

Remembering his first days as principal, Mr. Kamm says, "I had a large art and science room, where projects could be left out. It was here that children explored hands-on projects in science and made pinch pots out of clay."

He knew the owner of the bowling alley, who offered him aquariums for the school. He filled one tank with local fish—channel and flathead cat. Another tank held a piranha, and one was stocked with guppies. These were placed in the science/art room. Each classroom also had an aquarium that held neons and angelfish.

Believing that it was important for each child to have something to observe and care for, Mr. Kamm took large empty glass jars from the cafeteria, cut off the tops, and sealed them. He put guppies in them and gave each child his or her own aquarium to take home.

"I showed them how to feed the fish and care for them," he says. "They were an endless source of interest and delight for all of us. The only experience I didn't share with them was the feeding of the piranha. I did that after school."

FROM PRINCIPLE TO PRACTICE

Mr. Kamm believed that good teachers promoted a sense of family within their classes, and that the principal created a sense of a wider family for the entire school. This included mothering or fathering all the students, valuing children as individuals, and caring for one another, students and faculty alike. He believed in building traditions for students to anticipate and memories that would stay with them throughout their lives. He allowed students and faculty the latitude to learn, and didn't judge others' lack of information or expertise.

TO CONSIDER

As the father or mother of your own school, what experiences would you share with your students? What places of lifelong learning do you visit frequently? How might you make these places accessible to the children in your school? How might you extend these opportunities to an entire school? What is the most rewarding aspect of teaching, for you personally? In what ways will the nature of these rewards change, if you move to school administration? How might you preserve the valued aspects of teaching as part of your educational leadership?

6

NOTICING AND
THE LOOK

"First of all," he said, "if you can learn a simple trick, Scout, you'll get along a lot better with all kinds of folks. You never really understand a person until you consider things from his point of view . . . until you climb into his skin and walk around in it."

—From *To Kill a Mockingbird* (Lee, 1960, p. 30)

School teachers have always used the "look" to get students' attention, change inappropriate behavior, or silence a class. Sometimes it just expresses annoyance or exasperation. Other times, it threatens, with the unspoken "Do you know what will happen, if you persist?"

Students respond to the "look" in various ways, depending on their individual temperaments and past experiences with the teacher. Some looks are ignored, others defied. At best, they gain compliance, either from fear of the consequences implied or embarrassment of being caught in the act.

Mr. Kamm's "look" said something else. It was used sparingly, but precisely. Students from his first to last days of teaching report that the "look," at its best, expressed expectation—"I know you can do this." At its worst, it conveyed disappointment—"You can do better than that. I know it."

Noticing was not confined to the classroom. Although Mr. Kamm might be engaged in a focused activity, nothing seemed to escape him that might require attention. Inside and outside the school, in the classroom or on the playground, he noticed constantly—individual children, groups of children, his faculty, parents, and school visitors. But not overtly.

He did not stare to intimidate, but rather to remind, when a transgression was in the offing. He could catch the eye of a child across an entire playground and gain almost immediate compliance.

He also watched to see who might be feeling left out of a game, and moved to that child's side, paying him or her some attention. Observing a tired or demoralized teacher, he might tell an amusing story or take his or her class outside to hunt four-leaf clovers or play kickball. Harried parents were invited into his office, where he listened sympathetically to their concerns.

From the time Mr. Kamm greeted the school buses, he monitored children as they descended the steps, noticing moods and responding to greetings, sometimes giving a pat on the head. After recess periods, he looked for signs of physical or emotional distress, and often cut off problems before they escalated.

Who was too upset or energetic to enter the classroom? Who looked too warm, or overly chilled? Who should get a drink or use the washroom to clean up? Who needed a word of encouragement or just a little attention? He spoke to these children. He noticed them all.

The responses of students were instant. Their eyes lit up, they smiled or confided. They had value. Mr. Kamm, the principal, was talking to them. He was interested in what they had to say.

Mr. Kamm ate in the cafeteria with the students and then walked among the tables, commenting as a father might about untouched vegetables. "You need to eat a few more of those green beans," or "Drink your milk. It makes strong bones." He reminded students of their table manners and entertained them with jokes and puns. His presence minimized distractions that ordinarily plague school cafeterias.

Teachers invited Mr. Kamm to their classrooms frequently, to see both small successes and grand productions. He sat in the back of the room, almost unnoticed with his quietness. Children and teachers could sense him noticing and were inspired to their best performances. Sometimes he joined a class to listen to a story being read out loud to them, enjoying the experience as much as the children.

Many times, he told the class what he had observed, commenting on what was remarkable, excellent, or surprising. Sometimes he sat in class to notice other things. Did an individual student upset the dynamic of the classroom in a negative way? How did the teacher interact with this student? How did other students respond?

He watched, thought, and observed some more. What might help? He would later meet with the teacher, and at this point, the problem then became *their* problem. The teacher was spared the isolation and fear that often accompanies classroom unrest.

When Mr. Kamm entered a classroom without an announced purpose, children noticed back. Why was he there? Were they going outside to look for four-leaf clovers or arrowheads? Were they too noisy? Was he going to read to them?

In strolls past classroom doors, Mr. Kamm watched for teachers who might be distressed and needed a breather. He watched to see if the children were unusually rambunctious and needed an outing.

"The wind is right for flying a kite," he might announce, and out the door they would all go for an unscheduled science lesson. They observed the direction of the wind, the amount of string used, and the optimal way to face the kite for lift-off. What made the kite fly? What kept it in the air?

He had a third eye for other people's feelings and could sense pain, even when it was heavily concealed. When he speaks of any regrets in his long career, it is of those times when he saw the behavior and missed the pain. According to those who know him well, this was a rare event.

FROM PRINCIPLES TO PRACTICE

Mr. Kamm made it a practice to notice children, to be aware of their states of mind and behavior. He recognized them as individuals—learned their names, remembered their birthdays, knew what they enjoyed, and talked to them about it. This practice helped develop bonds of trust and built a foundation of self-esteem in his students. Acting-out behavior was often prevented because Mr. Kamm gave immediate attention to despair, as he supported self-confidence and courage. He observed without judgment, and focused on solutions, rather than punishments. This approach, according to Mr. Kamm, helped him participate in the renewal of spirit, including his own.

TO CONSIDER

How aware are you of the changing moods of your students and coworkers? Do you see yourself as someone able to provide encouragement and direction when teachers or students experience distress or failure? Do you feel comfortable addressing problems directly? Are you hesitant to judge, and patient with slow progress? How well do you involve others in solving problems of mutual concern?

7

QUOTH
THE CHILDREN:
"READ SOME MORE!"

There is no frigate like a book, to take us lands away . . .

— Emily Dickinson (1957, p. 13)

Mr. Kamm believed that reading should be enjoyed for its intrinsic rewards, not to earn credits for pizza, or to see the principal kiss a pig when the students had read 1,000 books.

He read aloud every day to his own class of fifth graders, wanting them to "feel the power and gentleness of the flow of language." Mr. Kamm shared the best of classical literature and poetry with his students, believing that "kids have a natural love of words, rhyme and rhythm. The music of poetry capitalizes on this love and helps it grow."

He also read aloud to other classes on a regular basis. "I wanted *all* kids and the teachers to know that I thought reading was important—that I enjoyed it and wanted to share that joy."

"As a teacher and principal," he says, "I believed strongly in the importance of reading aloud to children. When we shared the joy of reading, the joy was mine *and* theirs. I saw it as an opportunity, not an obligation."

"More importantly, I believe that reading aloud provides continuity to our lives, as we pass along our ideas and ideals from parent to child, teacher to class, generation to generation, and age to age."

Two anecdotes illustrate the way Mr. Kamm used reading aloud, both for the sheer delight it provided him and his students, and for the way it also served other purposes. The first is from the author's observation of Mr. Kamm when he read aloud to the kindergarten class.

He was always alert to the units of study in each classroom, and offered assistance to teachers in whatever form they found helpful. One morning, Mrs. Nave, the kindergarten teacher, asked if he would like to read Eric Carle's *The Very Quiet Cricket* (1990) aloud to her class that afternoon. Mr. Kamm took the book, promised to look it over, and show up after lunch.

At the appointed hour, he sat down in a small chair, at eye level with the children gathered around him. He showed the students the front cover of the book, and asked them if they had read other books by this illustrator. Almost as one, they turned and pointed to the book rack at the back of the room.

"*Rooster's Off to See the World!*" (Carle, 1999) they replied, excitedly. "Eric Carle!"

Mr. Kamm talked briefly with the children about the cover of the book, and made complimentary remarks about the insect pictures they had made, using a tissue paper collage, similar to Carle's.

The book was a hit, and the children begged Mr. Kamm to read it again. After the second time through, he asked them questions about crickets and insects: Are crickets insects? Are insects animals?

As he got ready to leave, one of the boys said, "My brother pulls the legs off of crickets."

"Oooh!" the girls groaned, making faces.

A few of the boys whispered, "Cool!"

"What do you think about that?" Mr. Kamm asked him.

"I don't do it," he replied.

The principal patted him on the shoulder. One of the boys who had said "Cool!" caught Mr. Kamm as he started to leave the room.

"I wouldn't do that either," he said.

"Good for you, Kevin," the principal said. "I didn't think you would."

No moralizing occurred in this exchange, but it's likely that neither boy forgot it. The interaction allowed the class, and more particularly, the two boys, to safely examine their values in Mr. Kamm's presence.

The first boy wanted an opinion about something he'd seen happen. The second wanted Mr. Kamm to know that his first response ("Cool!") was not the way he really felt. Both were reassured that Mr. Kamm knew they would do the right thing. Reading aloud provided the principal with many opportunities for these kinds of exchanges.

Mr. Kamm described what happened when a book of Edgar Allan Poe's writings showed up at school in the hands of a child who had difficulty being accepted by her classmates.

> Lee had been in my class for several months, but peer acceptance of her was minimal. One day she arrived, clutching a well-worn copy of Poe's writings. She had discovered "The Raven" and wanted to share it with me. I had not previously read this poem to my class—again I underestimated their love of language.
>
> They were fascinated by Poe's musical, mystical melancholy. "Quoth the Raven: Nevermore" became their spontaneous choral response as we read the poem several times. I needed no teacher's guide to lead us; the class's natural interest and curiosity served far better. Lee, and her book, through her book, became part of us. (Popp, 1996, pp. 56–57)

Once a child who had been sent to the office to spend some detention time brought along a book to read. Mr. Kamm had read the book, and they talked about it together. From the discussion, he formed a bond with the child that enabled him to understand her better and work on the causes, and not the symptoms, of her misbehavior.

After this experience, Mr. Kamm asked teachers to send a book along with children when they were sent to the office. "I wish I had known about this a long time ago," he said. "I think I could have helped more children."

Asked to write about why he enjoyed reading aloud so much, Mr. Kamm described the experience of reading *The Pied Piper of Hamlin* to his class of fifth graders:

> The Pied Piper marched into our classroom much as he must have entered Hamelin Town hundreds of years ago, cloaked in language as foreign to our ears as his strange garb had been to the eyes of the Hamelin people. But through the lilting language of Browning, the Piper charmed us and led us, as he had so many others before.
>
> True, we stumbled and hesitated along the way, but the pen of a powerful storyteller led us through the obstacles. And how, like the rats and the children, we raced through the lighter passages! (Popp, 1996, p. 57)

FROM PRINCIPLES TO PRACTICE

Mr. Kamm believed that reading aloud exposed students to types and qualities of literature they might not otherwise experience. It created a bond among students, and between students and teacher, to share a book together. He believed that reading aloud to students modeled an interest and enthusiasm for reading, which he regarded as the cornerstone for all learning.

TO CONSIDER

Do you enjoy reading all types of literature? What kinds of books do you share with others—your family, friends, students? If you are teaching, do you have a classroom library? What value do you see for principals to be knowledgeable about the current literature published for children? How comfortable would you feel if you were asked to read aloud in each of the grade-level classrooms in your school? What classical literature might you share with students, to which they might otherwise not be exposed?

8

PHONE HOME, THEN WIPE THE SLATE CLEAN

A person who is trained to consider his actions, to undertake them deliberately, is . . . disciplined. Add to this ability a power to endure in an intelligently chosen course in the face of distraction, confusion, and difficulty, and you have the essence of discipline.

—John Dewey (1985, p. 136)

It was Mr. Kamm's practice to invite each new student to the office to get acquainted, often with milk and cookies. He wanted their first visit to be a pleasant one, so that if worse came to worse, a bond of trust and not fear would already have been established.

Mrs. Nave, coteacher with Mr. Kamm in the fifth grade and later the kindergarten teacher, says, "He was someone admired enough by students and teachers alike, that living up to his standards of teaching performance or student behavior was a goal shared throughout the school."

"But it wasn't 'his' rules or 'his' way of doing things that drove this desire to achieve," she continues. "He encouraged and supported new methods of teaching that teachers wanted to try, and efforts of children to achieve in ways they had previously experienced difficulty with."

Mr. Kamm was his faculty's and students' biggest cheerleader when they took risks, and their most sympathetic comforter if things didn't turn out as planned. He sought opportunities to learn and grow himself, and supported all efforts by his staff or students to do the same.

Mr. Kamm's rules were succinct and easy to remember: "Don't bring anything to school or act in any way that is dangerous, destructive, or distracting." He said that this rule was sufficient, because it covered everything from porn to nuclear bombs.

He had a "one-warning" rule for misconduct that involved behavior that was unacceptable, but not harmful to other students or faculty. With more serious offenses, such as fighting or verbal abuse, there was no warning, but everyone knew the consequences of this behavior from the first day of school.

The one-warning rule involved misdemeanors, such as bad language.

"You don't want to have to call your mother and tell her that you said that, do you?" he'd ask.

This was often enough to stop the behavior immediately, or at least put the student on guard. If the offense was repeated, students had to call their mothers and tell them what they had said.

"If it was good enough to say at school, it was good enough to tell Mama," Mr. Kamm said.

A former student recalled, "It was worse than a spanking."

Mrs. Nave said of Mr. Kamm's discipline that "he was firm and to the point, but after an episode, he forgot about it and went on. Everyone had a new beginning." She added, "He was his students' biggest fan."

"One was not afraid of Mr. Kamm. He was not a punisher," she adds. "One only feared disappointing him."

This sentiment echoed the experience of a former student, almost to the word. He said that he dreaded going to the office, not because he was afraid of Mr. Kamm, but because he was ashamed to face someone who thought he could do better.

When older children misbehaved, Mr. Kamm told them: "You don't want the younger kids to see you doing or saying that and thinking it's okay," he said. And then the clincher—the ultimate vote of confidence: "I know you don't."

Of his approach to discipline, he said: "I laid out the consequences of actions and expressed a sincere belief that they would do things the right and responsible way. But if I said something would happen, it happened."

"Discipline was individual, on a case by case basis," he says. "I have some regrets. If I'd known what I later knew, I would have handled things differently." The sentiment of all conscientious educators.

Teachers spoke of his efforts to support them and help them do their best in the classroom. If an episode met with his disapproval, he was direct about it, offered assistance, and then everyone went on with a clean slate.

Because he spent little time in his office, Mr. Kamm knew what was going on in all the classrooms and was often able to intervene before bad things happened. When irate parents appeared at the door, he ushered them into the office, where he listened carefully to complaints. Later he dropped by the teacher's room, gave them a heads-up on any potential problems, and offered help, if that was needed.

A mild-mannered gentleman, he once took the arm of an angry parent who was threatening a teacher and firmly led her out the door, with the admonition to return when she could show proper respect.

In word and deed, Mr. Kamm spoke and lived his ideals. A former student tells how he and his teammates were influenced by Mr. Kamm's standards during a basketball game with a team from a neighboring town. The other team's coach swore loudly enough to be heard by the players.

Mr. Kamm walked over and asked him to refrain. When the profanity occurred a second time, he told the coach he would concede the game and take his players from the floor, if the swearing continued. He was willing to lose the game to win the high ground, and his players never forgot.

He wanted to model for his students that when others fail to act responsibly, it's better to walk away. A student later said this advice influenced him not to drive with a fellow high school student who had been drinking. He was spared being in a near-fatal car accident.

In some schools, failure to produce homework assignments on time merits a zero, regardless of excuse, and the work cannot be made up. At Summerfield, there were always second chances. Mr. Kamm and his faculty provided an additional day to complete the work, believing that it was counterproductive to deny students the opportunity to learn the information or skill.

In some educational psychology courses, teachers in training are taught to ignore troublemakers, because behavior will stop if it is not reinforced. A frequent diagnosis of acting-out behavior is: "They're only trying to get attention."

Mr. Kamm agreed that children who caused trouble were indeed trying to get attention, and he gave it to them. He paid attention to them when they were not misbehaving. He talked to them in the hall, on the playground, and downtown, if he met them there. He included them on nature walks, and let them know that someone cared—that someone was indeed paying attention.

FROM PRINCIPLES TO PRACTICE

Mr. Kamm modeled, in his own behavior, the values he wanted his students to acquire, believing that what he did spoke louder than words. He was clear about the consequences for certain behaviors, but allowed for mistakes and extenuating circumstances. He expressed belief in a child's best efforts and provided for new beginnings. His teachers also got the benefit of the doubt. When mistakes were made, the problem was resolved, and then forgotten.

TO CONSIDER

What value do you see in getting to know the students in your school *before* a disciplinary action might be warranted? Do you agree with Mr. Kamm's practice of giving everyone a fresh start after a mistake? Some school districts have discipline policies set down by boards of education or superintendents. If your experience with effective discipline differed from what was mandated by your district, how might you approach the board or a higher administrative authority to gain permission to maintain an approach that was different, but effective, for your particular school?

9

THE DAY CHARLIE GOT HIS NEW TEETH

I am proud that I have been a teacher. Teaching is something above and beyond teaching lessons and facts from books. It is this, but more too. It is helping a youth to find a path of his own that will eventually lead him through fields of frustration and modern pitfalls of destruction until he finds himself.

—Jesse Stuart (1958, p. 7)

Long before public policy demanded equal educational opportunity for all children, regardless of physical or mental ability, and decades before inclusion became an educational mandate, everyone was included in the classrooms at Summerfield. From kindergarten on up, students and teachers welcomed children with disabilities as interesting, not odd, members of the community.

Mr. Kamm believed that it was everyone's job to respect and care for one another at school. All children had special needs. Some needs were more apparent or demanding than others, but each child was to be taught to his or her full potential, challenged to take risks, and assisted when necessary.

Including children with disabilities in the regular classroom can be a stressful experience for many teachers. They might lack the information or training required to meet the challenge, or alternately worry that they are neglecting either the special needs child or the rest of their class.

Mr. Kamm briefed his teachers before these children came to school and made regular visits to the classroom to check on their progress. He made certain that teachers had adequate assistance to meet these challenges, provided information and moral support, and served as a liaison between parents and teachers, when there were difficulties. No teacher was left to deal with problems on his or her own.

As a consequence of his involvement in the full integration of special needs children in the classroom, teachers felt comfortable sharing their difficulties, knowing that they would have the help they needed to make the classroom facilities and learning experiences accessible to all their students.

Paul had epilepsy, which was only partially controlled by medication. One day, a kindergarten student met a visitor at the door and excitedly announced that she was Paul's assistant for the day.

"I get to bring him his pillow when he closes his eyes," she said, "and make sure he doesn't fall down." Then she added. "I cover him up with a little blanket and stay with him until he wakes up and feels better. Then I show him what to do, if he missed something."

Charlie was born with ectodermal dysplasia. Uncertain about his condition, his mother read, researched, wrote letters, and called experts until she found diagnosis and treatment. To share her knowledge and experience, she founded the Ectodermal Dysplasia Foundation, and has helped hundreds of parents who need information on how to get an education for their children. Until her work began, these children were isolated and parents were often unable to cope.

When Charlie came to school with thin hair and no teeth or sweat glands, his mother was determined that he have the same educational opportunities as any other child. Charlie was an engaging charmer and was welcomed into the fold, where he explained his condition to the class, much like an explorer would recount an exotic trip to Africa.

In the classroom, he was treated like any other child. Perhaps he was valued a bit more by the teachers, because each year that he progressed in school brought the luxury of air conditioning to his new class.

When Charlie was fitted for dentures, it was a cause for celebration in the kindergarten class. "Charlie got his new teeth!" children exclaimed to visitors, and pulled them into the classroom to have a look. "Come see them!" they cried. "They're wonderful! He can take 'em out and put 'em back in!"

Charlie's new teeth were a hit. Charlie later won the geography bee in fifth grade and continued on to college.

Kate was the daughter of Ingrid Patterson, the third-grade teacher. She was born with cerebral palsy, and attended classes at Summerfield on a limited basis. Later, when she was tutored at home, Kate was included in every field trip taken by the school. Lively, intelligent, and alert, she participated in the school's activities to the fullest extent possible. Kate, a talented artist, was always a part of the school family.

Mr. Kamm says that he encouraged his students to listen carefully to words, to hear the sounds that would help them spell correctly. "But I learned something new," he says, "when Kathy transferred to Summerfield from the Central Institute for the Deaf."

"She lip-read and taught me how to teach her," he says. "In fifth and sixth grade she contradicted my 'always sound it out' rule, by never missing a word. Kathy taught me not to turn my back when I was talking, not to mumble, and to face people when I talked. She taught me that there is always another way of doing things."

Mr. Kamm remembers Rick, who "spent a few months of his eighth-grade year on a chaise lounge, stretched out with a full-length cast on a broken leg. His classmates took care of him better than we could," he says. "And then there was James, who came to school in an electric wheelchair. He was very self-sufficient, and I just stayed out of his way!"

Barney, born with spina bifada, came to Summerfield for seventh and eighth grades because he couldn't manage the steps at Lebanon Grade School on his crutches. "Barney was amazingly self-sufficient and very personable," Mr. Kamm says. "The only accommodation was to provide him some privacy in the restroom."

"Jim Furtkamp was homeroom teacher for both Barney and Rick, and did a superb job of fitting all his students into the class. He concentrated on ability, not disability."

"Deb Cryder (Title I intermediate teacher) was our leader in accommodating kids with learning disabilities," he adds. "Her emphasis, like Jim's, was on ability, not disability."

Hayley had a form of muscular dystrophy and came to kindergarten with a walker. After a few weeks, she discarded it, and joined in with most of the activities of the other children. By the fourth grade, other students helped her with necessary activities, as a matter of course. When subjects changed, Hayley's book would be out on the desk and ready, under a watchful classmate's eye. Others helped her change her shoes for gym or perform tasks as needed.

Mark had multiple sclerosis, but was an active member of his study teams. Handwriting was difficult for him, but he persevered. The teachers could read what he wrote, and he excelled. The only accommodation necessary for him in the school routine was PE, and he selected the activities in which he could successfully participate.

Curtis had Asperger's syndrome, a type of autism. Teachers reached out to him—he loved to be hugged, but could not meet their eyes. Routines were key to his sense of well-being. If a subject was missed because of a classroom visitor, he was clearly upset. But teachers reassured him that the schedule would return intact the following day, and things would be as they always were.

In fourth grade, he memorized the order of all 30 spelling words each week, and often finished writing before dictation was completed. "How do you do that?" Mrs. Parker asked him.

"I don't know," came the reply.

His classmates began to ask him "What's the next word?" Curtis would smile and accurately provide the correct word.

Mrs. Parker says that he could immediately locate errors in handouts or things written on the board. "Good!" she told him.

He felt valued. Curtis was also an artist of some skill, and received recognition for his work.

When children transferred into Summerfield School, they sometimes lacked the skills to enter a particular grade. Some were placed at a level where they could be successful, and promoted as they developed the ability to achieve successfully. Others were given extra help by student tutors, the Title I teachers, and faculty volunteers to help them catch up to their classmates. Parents were encouraged to be patient with the progress made, and in most cases, students caught up by the end of the school year.

When students with disabilities came into Mr. Kamm's care, he told them that they were responsible for telling him or their teachers what they could or could not do. This approach deflected unwanted assistance, provided a measure of dignity, and in most cases seemed to motivate the children to do the best they could. They often took positive risks and achieved at a level beyond what their parents had thought possible.

Deb Cryder and Kay Dunn (Title I primary teacher) assisted the regular classroom teachers with programs that supported developmental reading and math. Marilyn Skingly, a full-time teacher's aide, assisted in several classrooms and shared her musical talents with all the grades. These teachers were integral members of the school family and frequent visitors to the regular classrooms. They were greeted as familiar instructors by all children, regardless of title program placement.

Although all of his students believed that Mr. Kamm was their friend, each felt that he or she was someone he knew personally. As he speaks of his former students, it is evident that Mr. Kamm *did* know each one as an individual. He remembers their high and low times, their successes, and the times they were challenged. He speaks with pride of their accomplishments, or of the tragedies that later befell their young lives. He shares the humor and joy that each brought to him.

When families experienced grief, through death or illness, Mr. Kamm counseled parents to send their children back to school. "Let them be children during the day—experience the normal and familiar—and put themselves back together again."

For other children, the school family was the only constant in their lives—a place where they were comforted and cherished, in ways that were sometimes not possible at home.

Mr. Kamm believed that "a good teacher brings children out of themselves and helps them find their niche in life. With some children, this niche must be built from scratch. For others, it is a process of improving or redirecting energy and skills."

The goal, in his words, was to "discover, develop, encourage, honor, value, and dignify each child in our care." This was a tall order, but former students, their parents, and his faculty believe that this goal has been achieved in ways that continue to unfold in children's lives, long after their time at Summerfield.

FROM PRINCIPLES TO PRACTICE

Mr. Kamm realized that successful inclusion of children with special needs in the regular classroom required careful planning and preparation. Teachers were not left alone to face these challenges, but were supported with necessary accommodations for physical or emotional problems and learning difficulties. He shared the responsibility for these children, as he did for all the others in his care.

TO CONSIDER

Have you worked with children who face challenges to full participation in the classroom—physical or learning disabilities, social or emotional problems? What kinds of support did you either receive or hope for if special needs children were included in your classroom? Of what value might it have been to have the principal's support and involvement in this situation? As principal, how would you assist teachers who are overwhelmed by the demands of inclusion?

10

IF THE COOK
DOESN'T SHOW UP,
BOIL SPAGHETTI

Our society cannot achieve greatness unless individuals at many levels of ability accept the need for high standards of performance and strive to achieve those standards within the limits possible for them. . . . [W]hoever I am or whatever I am doing, provided that I am engaged in a socially acceptable activity, some kind of excellence is within my reach.

—John W. Gardner (1961, pp. 131–132)

Mr. Kamm believed that all work had value in a school community, and modeled this belief in his everyday behavior. At the beginning of his career, the young principal received word that the cafeteria cook would not be coming to school that day, because she was ill. There were no substitutes in those days, and there were hungry children to feed.

"I just boiled up some spaghetti, put some sauce on it, made buttered bread sandwiches, and that's what we had for lunch," he says.

Mr. Kamm was a firm believer in the nobility of all work that serves a community. He mopped up snow from the floors or water overflow from the restrooms when the custodian was busy elsewhere. He believed that no work was beneath any man, and that he had no right to expect others to do work that he was not willing to do.

He hoped to model the idea to students that the school was everyone's home, and it was everyone's responsibility to keep it neat and clean. When graffiti found its way onto the playground or the sidewalks, he took a bucket of water and a scrub brush outside to clean it up. Soon, the students joined in. If the appearance of the school grounds was important enough for the principal to be on his hands and knees cleaning it up, they wanted to do the same.

When he was questioned about the dignity of a principal mopping up the floors, he responded that people dignified themselves more by pitching in and doing things. This approach to problem solving was adopted by his faculty. When a teacher went home sick, her class was quickly folded into another, and lessons went on with little interruption. When the cafeteria cook was absent, all pitched in to serve food and wash up the dishes.

To help students develop a sense of responsibility, Mr. Kamm paired up older children with preschoolers for field trips. The young ones felt protected and thrilled to have their own "big kid" for a buddy, and the older ones discovered a sense of nurturing they might not otherwise have experienced.

These events were chronicled in the *Lebanon Advertiser*, in the students' own words, beneath captioned photographs taken by Mr. Kamm. After a trip to the St. Louis Symphony and the St. Louis Zoo, Lauren described her experience for the newspaper:

> I think that bringing the pre-kindergarteners was an excellent idea. Most older kids like to watch little kids and answer their questions. I liked my child, Tiffany. She was a very, very good kid. She listened to what I told her and asked me a lot of questions. When we went to the living zoo at the St. Louis Zoo in Forest Park, we watched a movie of all the animals. Tiffany got scared, but I told her "That's just what animals do." Later we went to the St. Louis Symphony. We listened to *Beauty and the Beast*, something by Mozart, and a play of Peter and the Wolf. The pre-kindergarteners loved the play. I think we should bring them again.

Derrick, delighted with the responsibility of caring for a small child, while he had a new and exciting experience, wrote:

> The trip was exciting, because we got to act like parents. We took care of the preschoolers like parents. The fifth grade got to do *everything* like a parent. We went to the zoo and to the symphony hall. That was one of the best experiences of my life.

"Book Buddies" was a regular event at Summerfield. Second graders read to kindergarten children and first graders were read to by students in the fourth grade. Each group visited and read in each other's classrooms and explained any projects or displays they were working on. The older children's reading skills improved, and they became increasingly protective of their younger Buddies on the playground.

Every day, the entire school participated in SSR (silent, sustained reading). Children from kindergarten through fifth grade picked up a favorite book and read for 20 minutes. Mr. Kamm observed this ritual, as did all the teachers, and most of the staff. Immediately after lunch, a kindergarten child closed the door and put up a sign that read: "Please do not disturb. Children reading."

Sometimes, with the introduction of new students into the school, it was necessary to redirect their energy and transform their self-concept. A group of families moved to Summerfield from another state, bringing with them a different culture and children who had difficulty in school.

"We made a special effort to seek out the ones who needed help and tried to build them up," Mr. Kamm says. "We talked to them and paid attention to them. We made basketball players and readers out of them."

Mr. Kamm modeled problem solving to faculty and students by discussing issues with them and explaining the decisions he made. He listened carefully and approached opposing opinions with an open mind. He enlisted the ideas of others, and when decisions were finally made, he was always ready to provide the reasons for them. If he had made a mistake, he readily admitted it, and used new information he had gained to make future decisions.

The support staff at the school was also an integral part of the school family, providing services above and beyond what is usually expected. Joe Schmitt, the custodian, built shelves, easels, and other educational materials for the teachers. When it rained, he quickly went outside to make certain that all the teachers' car windows were rolled up. In the wintertime, he cleaned snow off windshields and warmed up the cars before it was time for the teachers to drive home.

Through the years, he unfastened children from tight spots, removing a step from the playground slide to free a trapped foot, and dismantling an entire desk to remove a boy who had somehow slid backward through the seat.

A former EMT, he was first responder for a child who had a seizure at school and rode with her in the ambulance to the hospital, so she would not be afraid.

Mrs. Nordmann, longtime school secretary, served as detention monitor when Mr. Kamm was not in the office and was also the school librarian. For many years, she opened the school library one day a week during the summer so children could check out books.

FROM PRINCIPLES TO PRACTICE

Mr. Kamm respected all honest labor that provided service for others. He treated his school like his home, and his students emulated this pride and respect in their own behavior. He enlisted the ideas and information of faculty and students in making decisions that affected the school and created opportunities for students to practice the rigors and joys of responsibility.

TO CONSIDER

How open are you to the ideas and experience of others? Would it be difficult to supervise teachers who are older than you, or more experienced in the classroom? What kinds of information and ideas might emerge from conversations with school maintenance personnel? Cafeteria workers? The school librarian or secretary? How comfortable do you feel about rolling up your sleeves to help out with things that need to be done around a school? Do you believe that good administration is limited to a strict delegation of responsibility?

11

MAKE AN EXPERIENCE
AN EVENT!

*What, then, is the true meaning of preparation in the educational
scheme? In the first place, it means that a person, young or old,
gets out of his present experience all that there is in it for him, at
the time in which he has it. . . . We always live at the time we live
and not at some other time, and only by extracting at each present
time the full meaning of each present experience are we prepared
for doing the same thing in the future. This is the only preparation, which in the long run, amounts to anything.*

—John Dewey (1991, pp. 29–30)

Each year, when Mr. Kamm and the teachers at Summerfield took children to the symphony in St. Louis for the Kinder Concert, they had
grand tier seating.

"If these children are going to the symphony," he said, "they will experience it in the finest way possible. If only once a year, they will be young
princes and princesses for a day."

Mr. Kamm sought experiences for his students that they otherwise might
not have. When a disgruntled parent asked, "Why do you take these children
to the symphony?" he answered simply, "Because you don't."

Many parents were surprised at the extent to which young children
soaked in the cultural learning that infused the curriculum at Summerfield.

One father told about the time his youngest son came home and talked about a Winslow Homer exhibit at the National Gallery of Art.

"How do you know about that?" his father asked.

"Mr. Kamm taught us," the boy replied.

The class had taken a fine arts summer field trip to the St. Louis Art Museum. The boy's father reported that he went out and bought the family a Winslow Homer print the following week.

Mr. Kamm believed it was his responsibility to take children into the broader world, to help them experience their culture and introduce them to places of lifelong learning and enjoyment. In the process, artistic appreciation reached out from the school into the community, as children described their experiences, and parents became involved in the trips as chaperones.

Mr. Kamm was a great believer in the dignity of artistic expression. When student art was displayed in the hall, it received gallery treatment.

"Having your drawings taped to the refrigerator is great," he said. "But having your painting matted and framed, and then displayed in a special place for all to enjoy gives art the dignity, respectability, and worth that it deserves. Kids see that art is part of life and that they can create it."

He also kept a glass display case in the front entry hall. It was a place to share rocks or bones the children discovered, a model they assembled, or a trophy won. "It was," he said, "a chance for them—any of them—to shine for a while by sharing something special. No matter what it was, it was special if it went into the display case."

One day, Mr. Kamm took his class mushroom hunting in the woods behind the school. It was a good day for morels, and the students brought back enough for a meal. He proposed that they fry up their bounty, but couldn't find any butter in the cafeteria kitchen.

A mother of one of the students says, "My son called me from school and asked me if we had any butter, and if we did, could I please bring some over to the cafeteria, because they were going to fry mushrooms!"

She took the butter to the grade school and watched many of the children enjoy their first taste of a delicacy they would seek out again and again, over the years.

Of this activity, Mr. Kamm said, "This was just a matter of sharing who I am—what I do, what I love—and passing it on. Any walk in the woods offers a time for sharing things—something that may not happen in the classroom for a child who is troubled—or just quiet."

Asked about a few of his more exciting moments as an educator, Mr. Kamm remembers: "We had a bus full of kids lunching on the steps below the St. Louis Arch, after a Kinder Concert at Powell Symphony Hall. The *Delta Queen* docked at our feet and serenaded us with a few numbers on the steam calliope!"

"After that, we walked the cobblestones beneath Eads Bridge to our appointment at the Dental Health Museum in Laclede's Landing. When we came out, the full hitch of Clydesdales were clomping down the cobblestone street, filming a commercial. What a day!"

"One year we had to cancel our annual field trip to St. Louis because of unrest in the city. We loaded up everyone on three buses—including the cook and the janitor—took along hot dogs and beans, and headed for the newly formed Carlyle Lake. Primary kids discovered brand new playgrounds, a sandy beach, and rode across the dam to Chipmunk Trail."

"The Governor of Illinois happened to be there and talked with the seventh and eighth graders for nearly half an hour," he says. "Then they were given a tour of the inner workings of the dam. My class (fifth and sixth graders) took a bus trip four miles up to Hazlett Park and discovered MORELS!"

In addition to trips made out into the wider community, Mr. Kamm and his teachers reached out and brought the community into the school—to share ideas, experiences, and performances. Christine Brewer, famed Metropolitan Opera star, graced the stage at Summerfield on more than one occasion. Personnel from nearby Scott Air Force Base shared their expertise in weather prediction. Every other year, visitors from the Wild Bird Sanctuary brought eagles, hawks, or owls for the students to observe.

An African American gentleman spoke to the fourth-grade class about his involvement in the civil rights movement. A Native American from the Cherokee tribe came to school in full ceremonial dress to demonstrate tribal dancing. Craig Virgin, world champion distance runner and Olympian, showed Summerfield students the Olympic torch he carried through the streets of Atlanta for the 1996 Games, and explained how it worked.

A woman, who was walking across the country to talk to communities about epilepsy, shared information about the condition with the entire school at Summerfield. As she continued her trip across the country, she frequently e-mailed the students, telling them all about the people she met and the places she was visiting.

Local farmers, beekeepers, big rig truckers, electricians, and community workers were invited to share their work and expertise with students. Demonstrations, exhibits, and performances brought the outside world into the classroom, and children learned that there was much to discover from everyone who visited.

Mr. Kamm shared many of his interests with students, but the main thing he shared was himself. He delighted in children's excitement when they discovered fossils, shells, and the coveted morel mushroom. He shared who he was with his students and enjoyed *their* interests, in return. He joined them on the playground, played with them, and observed what they enjoyed and did best.

Mr. Kamm took students on nature walks, where they hunted for fossils, skulls, and shells. Sometimes to help a young person discover something special, he would drop an arrowhead and brush dirt over it. Once, a student said, "This looks just like one I found last time."

Mr. Kamm observed, "Well, they look alike, sometimes."

Principals and teachers are frequently asked to join local service groups in a community, but Mr. Kamm chose his memberships carefully—avoiding activities and organizations he saw as exclusionary, divisive, or self-serving.

"For me," he said, "two hours a month circling the skating rink with a kid in each hand was far more productive than two hours with the guys at a local club meeting. Participation in school and all-community activities made me more visible to more people, and hence more approachable, and more likely to know what was going on."

Mr. Kamm believed that living in the community helped him to better know the students' backgrounds and their parents' expectations for them and the school.

"It gives you a stake in all that happens," he says. "You work *with*, not *for*, people—and vice versa. Successes and failures become *ours*, not mine, or his or hers or theirs."

In one of Mr. Kamm's favorite books, *Rising from the Plains* (1986), John McPhee comments on the advantages for geologists born and raised in Wyoming, where every strata of the earth's history is to be found.

In a similar manner, as Mr. Kamm grew up, he explored the physical geography, history, and culture of his own area of the country. He knew the rocks, trees, mushrooms, birds, and wildflowers. He also knew the people—from those who traced their roots to pioneer stock—to the newest arrivals.

This knowledge of the community, and the various cultures of which it was composed, helped him create a vision for school that was unambiguous: every child was expected to reach his or her highest potential. The best was expected from everyone. If talents weren't evident, they were searched for and discovered.

Although this familiarity with a place and its people was a great resource for Mr. Kamm's work as a teacher, principal, and superintendent, he would be the first to say that newcomers need not be outsiders. Like the geologist's mother, who arrived as a pioneer from the East in *Rising from the Plains* (1986), administrators willing to study a place and its people can be equally successful.

The operative word is *interest*. Mr. Kamm had a genuine interest in a community and its welfare—sincere concern for providing the best learning opportunities for the community's children and a willingness to be a vested member of the community itself, through participation in its customs, celebrations, and times of grief.

And the community responded.

Early in Mr. Kamm's career, Harrison Church, editor of the *Lebanon Advertiser*, gave the young Summerfield principal rolls of film and asked for stories about the school for his newspaper. The original copy, compared with the published news articles, shows that for 38 years, everything Mr. Kamm submitted about the activities of the school was printed by Mr. Church, without change. This allowed the principal to share the excitement and enthusiasm of school activities directly with the community, and kept citizens informed about what was happening in the school.

Mr. Church and his wife continue to support the activities at Summerfield School. They tell students how the great 19th-century author, Charles Dickens, visited Lebanon during a tour of America in the 19th century, and how the author of the classic *A Christmas Carol* commented positively about the hospitality he experienced during his stay in the historic town. They recently arranged for students to communicate with Dickens's great-grandson in England.

When the fourth grade studied the sinking of the *Titanic*, Mr. Church brought in old newspapers about the event and filled an aquarium with water and ice, so that children could place their hands in it to see how cold the ocean was for those trying to stay alive in the sea. Both he and Mrs. Church continue to read aloud to classes at Summerfield on Celebrity Readers Day, and participate in many of the other school/community activities.

Gail Nave says that her most treasured memory of Mr. Kamm's interaction with children was with Griswald, the class bear that went home with a different child each evening for a sleepover, accompanied with a journal.

"One day," the teacher says, "one of my students suggested that Mr. Kamm should have Griswald for a sleepover, which indicates how much they thought he was 'one of them.'"

"The rest of the class chimed in and thought this was a super idea. I then went to Mr. Kamm and made the request, which he graciously accepted. At the end of the school day, there was a knock on the door and we were asked to walk to his car."

"There sat Griswald, buckled up and wearing Mr. Kamm's sunglasses, ready to spend the night with Mr. Kamm's family. I can still hear the giggles of excitement when the children saw this."

"On Monday morning, Griswald and the journal returned, along with a beautiful storybook, complete with photographs and words, describing his adventures in the Kamm household."

"The following summer, Mr. Kamm took Griswald on vacation with him. When the next school year started, there was a new book, *Griswald Goes West*, a huge poster made from one of Mr. Kamm's great photo shots of Griswald in the mountains, and a small photo of Griswald made from the same print for each of the students."

She concludes, "What a zest he had for teaching and capturing the interest of his students!"

After reading the book *Rascal* (North, 1990) aloud to her fourth-grade class, Mrs. Parker sent home a stuffed toy raccoon named Rascal with a student every night. They reported the next day on Rascal's adventures in their home. She treasures a book made for her class, after Rascal visited Mr. Kamm's home on a weekend.

Titled *Loony Raccoony Limericks*, the book features nine colored photos of Rascal and accompanying limericks that describe his activities. Beneath a picture of Rascal, sitting beside a morel mushroom, is the limerick:

When Rascal and I hunt for fungus,
There's no other people among us.
We carefully walk,
And rarely we talk,
Lest we scare away one that's humongous.

Mr. Kamm believed it was important to be involved in the projects of individual classrooms. It was exciting for the students when the principal showed up, because they knew he would not only enjoy their presentations, but would have something to add, as well.

He once brought a basket of fortune cookies to share with the kindergarten, when they did the musical play *Tikki, Tikki, Tembo*. When the teacher told about his gift, she added that there were no Chinese restaurants or stores in the immediate area, which meant that he had to travel some distance to acquire the treats and provide this surprise for the children.

The school year was marked by celebrations and traditions that were anticipated from the time that children were old enough to be included in the school's activities. Some were just for fun, like Hat Day, where everyone wore an unusual or favorite hat to school. A variety of events celebrated Book Week, and trees were planted on Arbor Day. Mr. Kamm helped establish an Outdoor Education Day that was held each spring. The entire school spent the day at the YMCA Park, where students completed stress and obstacles courses and explored Fossil Hill.

A geography bee, spelling bee, and math contest were competitive. Mr. Kamm organized these events to "help students learn to strive, compete, win—or not win." His motto was: "Losing happens only when you don't try."

The principal also sponsored an art show and science fair, which he said, "gave students additional chances to share and shine in a setting more public than their classrooms." He believed that children's work was dignified by being presented in a form that honored its creator or discoverer.

Students, faculty, parents, and residents of Summerfield and Lebanon remember the school's traditional Pee-Wee Basketball tournament, the

Halloween Party, monthly skating parties, the Christmas Program, and Fun Day, which was celebrated on the last day of school.

"Everyone participated," Mr. Kamm said, "even in the basketball tournaments. Students who were not ballplayers or cheerleaders were timekeepers or kept score."

"These were all meant to be community events," Mr. Kamm observed, "often involving preschoolers to grandparents. They were opportunities for all of us to get together and share some kind of joy."

FROM PRINCIPLES TO PRACTICE

It was Mr. Kamm's practice to encourage children to discover their strengths, develop their abilities, and share them with others. He created traditions at Summerfield, with displays, open houses, parties, special events, and competitions. These celebrations were shared with the community, and the community responded by becoming more closely involved with the school.

TO CONSIDER

Every community has a different "heart"—a place where parents and children go to have fun together. How would you identify this place in the community to which you are assigned, if you entered as a stranger? How important is it to see and be seen by parents, students, and other members of the community? Do you have interests (music, photography, sports, crafts) that range beyond your work? How might you share these in a community setting?

12

YOU CAN'T DIRECT
THE WIND, BUT YOU
CAN ADJUST THE SAILS

*There is a fate that keeps alive in the world . . . the influence of a
good man; a fate that records him in others.*

—Mentor Graham, as cited in Duncan & Nickols (1944, p. 1)

The writings of Mentor Graham, noted teacher of Abraham Lincoln, are
limited to 20 recorded statements. Fire destroyed all of his books, letters, journals, and diaries. Lacking these primary sources, biographers exam-
ined the social and geographical contexts in which Graham had lived. They
rediscovered his life in the people who remembered his love of nature, his
bent for problem solving, and his desire to share what he knew with others.

People remembered the patience and perseverance of the frontier
schoolmaster—his dedication to his students, and his desire to improve the
lives of those he taught. Lincoln sought out Graham when he moved to
New Salem, Illinois, and worked tirelessly to learn everything he could
from the enthusiastic teacher. It was Mentor Graham who helped the
young Lincoln develop the disciplined habits of mind, which would later
be used to address the extraordinary problems of a divided nation.

In a similar manner, Charles Kamm was shaped by the world in which he
grew up—a social climate that encouraged young people to make a difference
in the world, a cultural climate that valued beauty and learning, and a physical setting that enticed its inhabitants to explore.

He spent much of his early life investigating the woods and streams around Lebanon. He played on slag piles and shale, discovering air tunnels and sink holes. Coal piles were combed for fern fossils and pyrite. From these experiences, he developed a lifelong love for geology. As an adult, he would dedicate his life to passing on these same interests to his students.

Mr. Kamm's mother, Hannah, was a German immigrant. She showed promise as an eighth grader, and could have gone into the convent school in nearby Belleville, but was sent out to work because of family finances. She valued education and drew, wrote, read, and played with her children, as she later did with her grandsons, Charles Jr. and Eric.

Mr. Kamm's father, Casper, was raised by his father and sisters, after his mother died in the 1917 flu epidemic. Education was important for him also, but he was forced to leave high school to work.

Mr. Kamm was one of four brothers, and the first in his family to graduate from college. With four boys in the family, there was a lot of activity around the Kamm home. Mr. Kamm remembers that a retired farmer passed their house every day, and on each occasion he told Hannah Kamm the same thing: "There's nothing worse than four boys, unless it's four boys and a mule."

Hannah Kamm's response is not on record, but she had great faith in the ability of each son to succeed. Mr. Kamm's eldest brother is deceased. Of his brothers who are still living, one is a neurosurgeon and the other a retired school teacher.

Mr. Kamm began teaching at Summerfield Grade School in 1955, when he was just 20 years old. He was drafted in the spring of his second year, but was allowed to teach until the school year was over. He chose 6 months active duty and 6 years active reserves. He was assigned to Camp Carson in Colorado, where he learned to love the Rocky Mountains.

At Summerfield, he taught fifth and sixth grades, trading English and science with the principal, who taught math and would later become the superintendent of Clinton County.

This principal was followed by one who absconded with the district funds and left his post early. He was followed by another principal in 1957, who had a fatal heart attack in 1961.

Mr. Kamm filled out the rest of the year as principal. "I figured I might as well," he said, "since people kept leaving and some weren't so good."

School yearbooks, family albums, and newspaper articles record the years of Mr. Kamm's teaching career. His earliest school pictures as a teacher show a tall, clean-shaven young man.

After his first year of teaching, Mr. Kamm entered active duty with the army. When he returned to finish the second half of the school year, photos showed him sporting a mustache, a feature that would be his trademark for the rest of his teaching career.

The Summerfield school yearbooks are a graphic record of Mr. Kamm's outdoor curriculum. In photographs, we see him fishing with students, marching in school parades, helping load children onto the school bus for field trips, examining farm machinery, and hunting for mushrooms, fossils, and rocks.

The camera followed him to school, as he read aloud to kindergarten children, awarded trophies, attended class plays, kept score for athletic competitions, and listened attentively to a firefighter, along with the kindergarten class, who were dressed out in construction paper fire helmets.

A photo shows Mr. Kamm standing on the grand staircase at Powell Symphony Hall in St. Louis, where reservations were made in advance, so all the children from Summerfield could have grand tier seating.

He seems to have been wherever people in the school gathered together: helping serve at PTA chili suppers, hosting Christmas parties and plays, visiting the nursing home with his class at Christmas time, celebrating Book Week, supervising the Young Authors competition, and digging holes to plant trees on Arbor Day.

This collection of photographs reflects a key value Mr. Kamm had for his teaching. He knew that children learned best from hands-on experience and exploring natural phenomena. Together, they explored and asked questions.

Mr. Kamm knew what was important and how to document it. He helped students and staff gain recognition and respect in the community by featuring their achievements in the newspaper and preserving significant events in pictures. The archives of the *Lebanon Advertiser* show the history of Mr. Kamm's influence on the community and its children, and constitute a time capsule of his years at Summerfield.

He also regularly nominated faculty for teaching awards. His teachers were recognized with regional, state, and national teaching excellence awards, including the Golden Apple, Illinois Teacher of the Year, and the prestigious Millkin Award.

In the *Lebanon Advertiser*, above pictures of fifth graders and their preschool companions, is the title: "Responsibility." In the photograph, older and younger children huddle together against a cold, wintry day in St. Louis' Forest Park. The little ones are bundled up like fluffy chicks, sitting on laps, being hugged, protected and shown a good time on a trip they will long remember.

Photo albums show Outdoor Education Day, with children looking at water features, examining rocks, balancing on beams, climbing, exploring, discovering, and learning. Many of the children had never been to an outdoor area of this size.

The kindergarten teacher had just read *Sarah, Plain and Tall* (MacLachlan, 1987) aloud to her class, and remembers: "Close by, there was a large, man-made lake, whose waters were green and shining. As we walked beside it, one of my most deprived students tugged at my sleeve and asked, 'Mrs. Nave, I wonder if this is the color of Sarah's sea?'" (Popp, 1996, p. 122).

He had never seen a lake before, but could now imagine the ocean.

In 1961, Mr. Kamm became both superintendent and principal for Summerfield Consolidated School District No. 1. He remembers the next 10 years as his best, when he was, as he says, "the superintendent, principal, teacher, scorekeeper, and occasional janitor."

In 1970 the district merged with the Lebanon, Illinois, schools, and Mr. Kamm became Summerfield's principal in Lebanon Community Unit District No. 9.

"This move," Mr. Kamm says, "took kids away from Summerfield and created a full-time principal, with more money and less to do."

This was not an acceptable situation for him. Mr. Kamm requested, and was granted, a part-time teaching assignment.

In 1974 the district moved children from the seventh and eighth grades to the junior high in Lebanon. With overcrowding at Lebanon and classrooms empty in Summerfield, Mr. Kamm proposed the volunteer busing of K–6 students to Summerfield. This would create even enrollments and balance the school populations, with regard to geography, race, and socioeconomic backgrounds. Although this decision was resisted by some at first, parents' written evaluations of the program after its first year indicate both acceptance and enthusiasm.

Earlier redistricting had also given Summerfield some students from St. Mary's Parochial School in nearby Trenton. The bitterness and disappointment among those forced to transfer to a new school did not last long, as principal and teachers welcomed every child, got to know each one as a person, and folded them into the Summerfield family.

In 2002 Mr. Kamm was inducted into the Lebanon High School Hall of Fame. The induction speech was written and delivered by Julia Parker, a longtime teacher at Summerfield. Of Mr. Kamm, she said:

> Mr. Kamm, you'll never know what an honor this is. When I informed my family that I was doing the presentation, my brother asked, "Is this the same one on your list of important people, where God is #1 and then there's Mr. Kamm?"

She praised her former principal for bringing a love of science to the school's children, and making it understandable to the teachers. She mentioned several art activities that he shared with students—making clay pots and necklaces, and drawing freehand, a copy of Picasso's *Hands Holding Flowers*.

Mrs. Parker expressed deep appreciation for the way he supported and protected his teachers:

> The students and staff of Summerfield knew he really cared about them. He always asked about our families and found something positive to say to us each week. It was not uncommon for him to buy a train book for a kid he knew loved them, to take a few kids for a Saturday fishing jaunt, or to the woods to hunt for mushrooms.
>
> He wore a green tie on St. Patrick's Day and read the story of Jeremy Bean (Schertle & Shute, 1987) to all the classes. The story was about a principal who noticed a student on St. Patrick's Day who was sad because he wasn't wearing green. So the principal gave him his green tie. Any teacher listening to that story knew that Mr. Kamm would have done the same thing.

Mrs. Parker also told the story of children coming to school one morning and discovering pennies on the front steps of the building. As the children came into school they picked them up and wondered how they got there. Mr. Kamm told them they were "pennies from heaven." He had thrown them there, after cleaning out his desk.

Perhaps the most telling tribute from this teacher is one that his other teachers would endorse equally: "Mr. Kamm, I want to thank you for making my job a pleasure to go to every day. It never seemed like going to work. You created a family atmosphere that all students and teachers could enjoy."

On the same occasion, Charles Kamm Jr. wrote to his father:

I want you to know what a profound influence you have had on my life and career choices. . . . I knew at Earlham that I wanted to become a musician, but my settling into teaching music, rather than strictly performing as a professional is due in large part to an idealized vision of what education can be—a vision formed at Summerfield Grade School and in seeing your work.

It is no mistake that I am working with mostly non-music majors in a liberal arts college, not with pre-professionals in a conservatory. It is a choice I have consciously made, and a choice grown out of my observations of your love of teaching—and learning—and its value to all people.

What were those traits in your work that so affected me? First, it was your commitment to teaching before administration, and your efforts to be a competent administrator. It always seemed to me that the role of principal and administrator was secondary and even subservient to teaching. This is as it should be; the administrator should really serve the educator, don't you think? I try to keep teaching foremost in all of my work (difficult at times, given how much administration there can be).

I have also always admired your willingness to be adventurous and deviate from the schedule and the textbook . . . to take advantage of the moment and of all the resources available to you. Field trips, science projects and rocket launches have translated for me into guest performances in class, singing a rehearsal in the chapel, rather than the choir room, or bringing in a new recording to share with the students, even if it doesn't bear directly on the music we are working on.

Another trait I think has colored my work is your deep sense of fairness and treating all equally—not only your students, but your teachers and even the parents. I know that you went into all interactions with an open mind, and kept that as long as you could. You always seemed to consider the other side of issues and how decisions might impact someone else.

Finally, your personal love of the subjects you taught and your caring for the students may be (as with all great teachers, I suspect) the greatest strength. I strive always to keep up that enthusiasm and concern. When all is said and done, I am deeply honored to have had you as a teacher, principal—and in many ways a mentor—as well as a father. You have influenced my life as a teacher greatly. And you have done much to form my humanity, as you have with so many others.

Enjoy tonight. I love you. —Chuck

The plaque presented to Mr. Kamm at the induction ceremony concluded with "Over the years, he has treated Summerfield School as his own family and has left a lasting imprint on the history of Summerfield School."

His presenter concluded her remarks with "You are, and always will be, 'Mr. Summerfield'."

The evening's presentations exhibited the influence of a good man in this community, for surely his life had been well recorded in the lives of others.

FROM PRINCIPLES TO PRACTICE

Few young people entering teaching or the principalship can imagine the number of lives they will affect. Their enthusiasm for learning, their sense of fairness, and positive regard for their colleagues will outlive them. It is an undertaking that requires skill, intelligence, patience, and courage. Most of all, it demands a love and kind regard for all people, and a willingness to become their best selves, through service to others.

TO CONSIDER

Working successfully with the media is a skill that is acquired over time. In a small town situation, editors are usually eager for print and pictures about school events. In larger cities, this relationship may require more effort—a personal visit to the education editor, or providing newspaper, radio, or television stations with a schedule of upcoming events. Follow-up calls, closer to the event itself, help remind editors of photo opportunities that can be of interest to the community. Does someone on your staff write exceptionally well or take good photographs? Enlist their skills. Providing your own copy in a timely fashion will help inform the community about the good things happening in your school, and work toward gaining support for the school's program.

13

IT'S NOT GOODBYE

I shall always treasure the joy of sharing thousands of days with hundreds of children. I like to believe that I gave them some of my love and excitement for learning. I believe it was what I was meant to do, and what I did best.

—Charles Kamm

It's a late spring day in 1993, and the Summerfield Grade School auditorium buzzes with talk. The voices of many children echo against the walls, where students are seated in long rows with their classmates. Mr. Kamm and his wife, Lynn, sit at the front. Their son Eric is at the gym door, camera ready. The mistress of ceremonies approaches the podium, and down the line, teachers hush their students, and everyone falls silent. It is time for the formal response to Mr. Kamm's retirement, which will happen at the end of the school year.

Mrs. Richter speaks of the honoree alternately with respect and humor. She is at ease, because she is Charlie's mother, and she's had to stand up to school boards and lawmakers to defend Charlie's right for an education.

She introduces Christine Brewer, noted soprano and opera singer, and mother of a fifth grader. Accustomed to the lavish sets of the Metropolitan and opera houses throughout Europe, she looks pleased to stand on the small school stage and sing to Mr. Kamm. Her commanding voice fills the gymnasium, and suddenly the venue is larger and more elegant. From *The Firestone Hour*, she sings the theme song, *If I Could Tell You*. The music and words are heartfelt and moving.

A small boy in a lime-green shirt and jean shorts sits backward on his chair, listening carefully; the other students are attentive. They have, after all, been to the symphony with Mr. Kamm since they were preschoolers, to hear as one young girl wrote, "something by Mozart."

At this point in the program, Mr. Kamm stands to recognize the talent and tribute. The PTA presents him with a silver picture frame, with room for photos in the back.

Students line up on stage and sing together. Tiny, clear voices ring out—some are sure of the words, others look around. A young boy in the front row puts his thumbs in his pockets. The children are a collage of sneakers, patent-leather shoes, jean shorts, dresses, bows, ribbons, barrettes, blonde, black, curly, and braided hair; skin of every hue.

Some children look directly at Mr. Kamm when they sing, others avert their eyes. One girl wipes a tear from behind her glasses. Suddenly the song is over. A fifth grader jumps from the stage, pulls out her camera, and takes a picture of Mr. Kamm. He smiles back at her.

Later in the week, it is finally the last day of school—the traditional Fun Day—and students gather to sing to Mr. Kamm once more. They burst out into song:

Through the years, you never let me down.
You turned my life around . . .

This time Mr. Kamm is seated at the back of the auditorium. The students turn around and sing directly to him, linking their arms around one another's shoulders, swaying back and forth comfortably, in the way children often do for parents when they vulnerably show their true feelings.

This was a love song, sung to the principal, the kind of humming lullaby that children sing when they feel happy, well fed, and safe. Mr. Kamm looked at each child, and each was the face of his own child, dear and familiar. "You wiped my tears away . . . ," they sang.

Among the tributes sent to the principal was one from an adult, who wrote that at her mother's funeral, where grief was everywhere, Mr. Kamm caught her eye and winked. "It was so reassuring," she said, "with Mr. Kamm, life goes on. People feel safe, cared for, and cared about."

Now the children march onto the stage and sing "Reach Out and Touch (Somebody's Hand)." They extend their arms to Mr. Kamm. Some of the boys are fifth graders, self-conscious and embarrassed by public displays of affection. They turn to grin at one another and twist around awkwardly as they forget the words and bump into one another.

A somber boy in the front is serious about singing. He knows the words and keeps still when he forgets. He brings to mind the slight, serious boy of long ago, who wanted to do things right, and grew up to do as many right things as he possibly could.

The younger children look back and forth, some unaware of being on stage; others have their hands in their pockets. The girls sing earnestly, lovingly—most know the words by heart. The more shy among them look down at their shoes as they stretch out their arms. Some are hesitant on the high notes, but all are singing with their hearts. It's in their eyes, the pitch of their voices.

Students introduce the songs. One girl says, "We love you, Mr. Kamm," as easily and comfortably as a child would say "I love you, Dad."

The students sing a lively rendition of "Gonna Stomp and Shout," with revival fervor—an emotional outpouring of energy and love. If the community program was a family reunion, this one was simply a large family, the head of which was being honored as a beloved father.

Each class has made a book for Mr. Kamm. They are the bound contributions of individual students, which combine art and creative writing. Some are alphabet books, which describe Mr. Kamm or his role as teacher and principal. Others use his name as an acronym:

K—You were always kind
A—You are amazing
M—You took us mushroom hunting
M—We will miss you.

Mr. Kamm stands, as the books are presented, and each class stands in turn, as the student representing them gives their class's book to him. He touches each child gently on the shoulder, and acknowledges the gifts graciously and warmly. A small fifth-grade girl reaches up and hugs him.

The program closes with "One Moment in Time" (. . . when I'm more than I thought I could be . . .). This moment in time cannot be captured in photographs or words, but in the warmth of the room. The final tribute is not even in the many gifts and tributes. Lives have been lived out differently for 38 years because of this man. Those moments in time will be alive for as long as these children live.

Later that day . . . a year later . . . and the year after that . . . 7 years later . . . a bell rings in the distance and a drum beat begins. Summerfield citizens wait on the sidelines for the last-day-of-school parade to begin.

The flag bearer leads off, with a guard to the right. A boy in the back of the formation begins a lively marching drum cadence, and the junior high band steps forward. They are well disciplined—eyes straight ahead and instruments held at parade ready.

Kindergarteners hold hands and wander off after the band. Their teacher works to keep them moving, as they look around at the people watching them. Each grade carries a large banner, announcing the class.

"First Grade Was Great!" one proclaims.

"4th Grade—Soaring into Fifth" reads another, complete with a giant paper eagle. Fourth graders follow the sign, carrying small American flags.

There are balloons and streamers on the banners; glitter paint and decorations. Red, yellow, blue, and green—the banners wave in the breeze. Children of every color, shape, and size add richness to the blend of students.

As the parade moves into the center of town, parents, siblings, and community members from Summerfield and Lebanon wait eagerly. Some of the little ones run to join the parade. Mr. Kamm takes the hands of two preschoolers and they march on.

Someone cheers the drummer and he flashes a bright, white smile. Two kindergartners sport caps and gowns. Mothers assisting the parade marchers hold children's hands to keep them from wandering off.

The crowd becomes increasingly vocal—cheering the marchers. Children call out to their parents on the sidelines. The tradition takes form and continues for one year more. Soon it will be time to launch the rockets. Mr. Kamm is still a part of this community's life.

FROM PRINCIPLES TO PRACTICE

The farewell programs for Mr. Kamm were consonant with the way he related to students, faculty, parents, and community members for 38 years. He had always included them in the activities and celebrations of the school, and now they enthusiastically became a part of the ceremonies that marked the conclusion of his full-time career as principal and teacher. No one said goodbye, because they knew Mr. Kamm would stay active in the community where he had lived all his life, and involved in the school he had served for his entire professional career.

TO CONSIDER

Of what benefit would it be to spend your entire career as teacher or principal in one school? In what kind of school or community would you feel most comfortable being an educational leader? If you were to serve in several different communities, what kinds of experiences would you bring with you to new situations?

APPENDIX A

SIT IN A BIG CHAIR
ALL DAY AND BOSS
PEOPLE AROUND

*Tell me how can good teaching ever die? Good teaching is forever
and the teacher is immortal.*

—Jesse Stuart (1958, p. 7)

Whoever you are in America, your life has most probably been influenced in some way by an elementary school principal. Principals enforce policies established by local boards of education, influence the morale of their faculties, and set the tone for the general conduct of their schools. These key functions of the principal directly affect the kinds of teachers who are hired and retained, the quality of the curriculum, and—as agents of learning—all students who pass through the school's doors.

If the school is a welcoming place, staffed with competent faculty and a principal who supports his or her teachers with resources and encouragement, it is likely that many of the students in their care will grow and develop into contributing members of society. And if these principals do their work exceptionally well, they will continue to be a positive force in these children's lives, long after they have left the school building.

A principal once asked the kindergarten class in his school if they knew what his job was. "You sit in a big chair all day and boss people around," came the reply.

Although this embarrassing portrayal might fit a small number of elementary principals, it does not begin to describe the endless responsibilities of the vast majority of conscientious educational administrators.

A principal's job is not an easy one. In addition to managing all the business of the school, working within a budget, and planning for growth, principals must also monitor the maintenance of a physical plant, provide for school safety, and assist in curriculum development. Principals evaluate teachers, interact with parents, and discipline students. They must work cooperatively with the school board and be the chief public relations officer for the media, and members of the political and business communities.

Each of these populations has different, and many times, conflicting expectations of the principal. If the job sounds too big for one person, that's because it is. Like teaching, the work of educational leadership expands to consume whatever time and resources are available.

THE WORD "PRINCIPAL" WAS FIRST AN ADJECTIVE

Originally, the position of principal was that of the *principal teacher* in a school—someone with experience and expertise, whom other teachers trusted. They could go to this person for advice and counsel about teaching, classroom management, and discipline problems.

But first and foremost, the principal teacher was a *teacher*, with a class of his or her own. This was the context in which they improved their craft, so that they had ideas to share. They often had more education, and attended classes or conferences, with the purpose of bringing back new and helpful ideas to the other teachers.

HOW DID WE GET *THE PRINCIPAL?*

The role of principal began in the late 1800s, when large city schools required someone to manage the school facilities, pay the bills, hire the teachers, and otherwise manage the enterprise of schooling. Initially, this person was a teacher who assumed more responsibilities for additional compensation.

But as city populations grew, so did the size of school buildings, student populations, and numbers of teachers. Increased responsibilities made it necessary to appoint a person who could devote all of his or her time to the management of a school. At this point, the educational leader moved from being the principal teacher to being *the principal*, and in the 1920s, educational administration became a profession of its own.

From the beginning, school administration required specialized training in leadership theory, finance, business management, teacher evaluation, physical plant maintenance, the preparation of schedules, and curriculum development. Principals were expected to create effective working liaisons with both the board of education and the community, to ensure maximum financial support and goodwill for the schools.

As urban teachers moved into this expanded managerial role of principal, the idea of the principal as head teacher was shuffled into the history books. There were too many constituencies to serve, and principals began to view teaching as a luxury they could not afford.

Rural school districts soon followed suit, and appointing principal/administrators to small town schools became the norm, despite the success of teachers who also served in the role of school manager.

WHAT IS THE PRINCIPAL *SUPPOSED* TO DO?

Over the years, the role of principal was shaped and reshaped by the expectations of school boards, schools of education, and professional organizations. In many cases, principals directed their practice from the models they experienced as students.

In the memories of many, principals were either invisible or intimidating. They stayed cloistered in their offices to reprimand the unruly, or roamed the halls to spot rule-breakers. On formal occasions, principals presided over school assemblies or student performances for the public.

New principals discovered that they weren't the only ones with preconceptions about what the principal ought to be doing. Parents demanded certain kinds of discipline, superintendents expected glowing test scores, the state and national governments sent mandates, and school boards were concerned with the bottom line. Ignoring any of these expectations jeopardized a working relationship with one or another of the principal's constituencies.

Some principals were willing to break the mold, because they believed their direct involvement in the instructional process was important to their faculties and students. They saw themselves as colearners in a community of learners that extended out into the community at large. Convinced that the principal should still be the principal teacher, closely involved in the instruction of students, many idealistic principals held fast to their instructional roots.

BACK TO THE BEGINNING

Eventually, educational researchers and the major professional organizations for administrators took notice of schools led by these principals. The code of the National Association of Elementary School Principals (NAESP, 2001) acknowledges the idea that the principal of an elementary school is a key figure in determinig the quality of education for students in their school. Principals are thus responsible for the progress and welfare of each student and are charged with helping all reach their full potential.

Recognizing the need to better describe and better educate elementary principals, the NAESP embarked on a study to redefine the role of the elementary principal as an instructional leader. In October 2001, they released a guide that reasserts the principal's role as the principal teacher and educational leader (NAESP, 2001).

This movement toward redefining the principal as the principal educator in a school is paired with a humanistic trend that sees the principal as the chief nurturer in a learning environment that includes students, staff, and the larger community, of which they are a part.

Current literature for elementary principals reflects this concern, with titles that describe a nurturing role for administrators (Lyman, 2000), and handbooks that outline the principal's role in creating learning communities (Norris, Barnett, Basom, & Yerkes, 2002) and implementing social-emotional learning (Pasi, 2001).

The word "caring" appears frequently in titles for educational leaders (Beck, 1994; Sernak, 1998), and articles in publications of leading journals for administrators stress the importance of creating a sense of community within the school, and inclusiveness among all participants in the learning process.

Stephen Covey (1991) identified eight characteristics of "principle-centered" leaders, describing them as persons who are continually learning and service-oriented. According to Covey, "they relate positive energy and believe in other people, trying to find the best in others, not their faults." "They lead balanced lives and enjoy a full range of social, intellectual, family and work-related experiences." Life is an adventure to these principle-centered leaders, Covey says. "Things that occur in their lives are challenges, not problems" (pp. 33–38). Jerry Patterson (1993) also discovered that principals who displayed these common behavior patterns could be equally effective, even though they differed from each other in personality or philosophy.

IT SOUNDS GOOD, BUT CAN IT BE DONE?

Do these publications and NAESP's ambitious re-creation of the role of principal simply add extra duties to an already unmanageable work load? Depending upon the particular talents and skills of individual principals, the standards might seem overwhelming. But the main tenets of the guidelines are something that good principals have managed to negotiate for years, long before it was professionally expected. From Sylvia Ashton-Warner (1986) in New Zealand to Jesse Stuart (1958) in Kentucky, educators have taken a good look at their resources and talents, and have brought them to bear on the task at hand.

Everyone acknowledges the influence teachers have on the lives of their students. People of celebrity and accomplishment often cite an influential teacher as someone key to their success. But there is an additional variable that is critical to the recruitment and retention of these valued educators— the principal.

Indeed, it is the professional trust of the principal that matters, when teachers are trying new methods to reach a diverse student population. It is the energy of the principal who cheers on discouraged or exhausted faculty and fights for the resources they need to do their jobs competently. It is the principal who sets the tone for a school that supports young children as they move out from their families into the wider world of the classroom and community.

In addition, the principles of the principal create a context where faculty are valued for the diverse talents they bring to teaching, and students are cherished as part of an extended family that will believe in them when they struggle and rejoice with them when they succeed.

Interested and involved parents and community members are critical; caring and competent teachers are indispensable. But it is the principal who sets the tone that will encourage all of these people to function at their best.

One can have parent involvement and an excellent faculty, but if the workplace is full of irrelevant or irrational expectations, interest falls off, teachers burn out, do the minimum expected, or leave. In the end, the principal plays a key role in determining if these resources will be put to their best and most profitable use.

WHAT DIFFERENCE DOES IT MAKE?

It would be fair to ask if nurturing principals leave a legacy to the schools they serve after they move on to other positions or retire. In Mr. Kamm's case, one might wonder what has happened to Summerfield School now that he is no longer its educational leader.

Many believe that the most accurate measure of effective classroom management occurs when the teacher is not in the room. This is the time when the teacher's influence on students is most strongly demonstrated. If the class continues to work quietly when their teacher is called out unexpectedly, they exhibit the efforts of that teacher to create an environment of autonomy. Conversely, if the room erupts into chaos, it is likely that classroom behavior has been enforced in ways that disintegrate, when the tenuous bonds of authority are removed.

Mr. Kamm's influence continues, more than a decade after his retirement, because he created an environment that encouraged his faculty, students, and the community to participate in decision making. In his absence, life at Summerfield Grade School continues in much the way as it did before he left, because the talents and professional performances of his faculty were developed and refined in response to a leadership style that was authoritative, without being authoritarian.

His teachers report that they so internalized his approach to teaching and learning that when difficult situations arise, they ask themselves, "What would Mr. Kamm do?" This isn't a statement of dependency, but rather a declaration of respect. Individual faculty members have grown and learned in the time since he left and have developed educational leadership styles of their own.

Many things have stayed the same. The approach to discipline is still to deal with the issue and then forget it. As was true during Mr. Kamm's tenure, all the teachers know every child. When one is having difficulty, the word goes out, and extra attention is paid to those having problems. Summerfield remains a large family, with concerned parents and a great many children.

High community involvement continues, as does the extraordinary support of the newspaper, which features the school's activities on a weekly basis. The Summerfield faculty still provides a variety of stimulating experiences for their students, both inside and outside of the school. As always, field trips include the custodian and the cooks.

The PTA continues to be an active and supportive influence at Summerfield. Parents volunteer their time in the classroom and participate in fundraising projects that supply a variety of educational materials to the school. Their work also helps provide extracurricular experiences for the students.

Christine Brewer, of opera fame, recently donated a substantial number of books about different cultures and different lands to the school, in appreciation for the school's contribution to her daughter's education. Elizabeth, now a college student, returned to Summerfield as a speaker for one of the school's cultural units.

Teachers bring in people to share with the entire school—authors and illustrators who live in the area, older people who remember historic events in the town, state, or nation's history. Classes still go to the symphony and the zoo. They divide up into teams to play in the Pee Wee Basketball Tournament, the most popular PTA fundraiser. They carry on Mr. Kamm's tradition of visiting the nursing home at Christmas time, to carol and visit with the people there. Joe Schmitt, the custodian, still leads the school in caroling before the class Christmas parties.

The daughter of the school's cook, who attended Summerfield School as a child, has taken her mother's place in the cafeteria. The great-nephew of Miss Elsie is student-teaching in fifth grade.

Celebrities still visit the school to read aloud to students. The program, "News Currents," initiated by Mr. Kamm in its first form as a film strip, provides fourth and fifth graders with enough knowledge about current affairs to draw comments from their parents. Test scores in social studies for these classes continue to be exceptional. When teachers have finished with the week's news, they give the programs (now on DVD) to the local senior center. Some report that they sense Mr. Kamm looking over their shoulders as they demand that all students learn to spell and use grammar correctly.

The legacy of Mr. Kamm's 38 years at Summerfield School is evident—in the spirit of his teachers, the traditions he helped establish, and the hundreds of students whose lives he influenced with his kind regard, constant encouragement, and enthusiastic teaching. In his absence, Mr. Kamm continues to influence the basic values of the school, through the key principles that guided his own instruction and administration. All who have known him are convinced that one man *did* make a difference.

FROM PRINCIPLE TO PRACTICE

Mr. Kamm modeled the elements of effective school leadership throughout his tenure at Summerfield. He gave his teachers opportunities to share in the decision making, which helped them develop and refine their own leadership skills. Because he had informed the community so well about the activities and vision of the school, they became a part of this vision and were highly motivated to carry on its traditions.

TO CONSIDER

What elements of your own leadership style would you like to share with a school? What ethical standards are important to you, as you work with children and the community of which they are a part? What legacy would you like to leave a school when you retire?

APPENDIX B

BIOGRAPHY OF CHARLES KAMM

I like to think that the greatest success of any life is that moment when a teacher touches a child's heart and it is never again the same. . . . Everything America is, or ever hopes to be, depends upon what happens in our school's classrooms.

—Frosty Troy (Chion, 2001)

Charles Kamm was born July 18, 1934, to Casper and Hannah Kamm, in the historic town of Lebanon, Illinois, across the street from the high school from which he would later graduate in 1952. During high school, he took classes at McKendree College, located just a few blocks away, and graduated from there in 3 years, cum laude, with majors in history and German. When he married, he moved to his present home in Lebanon, just across the street from the college.

Mr. Kamm earned a master's degree in educational administration from Southern Illinois University in 1966, and holds certifications in elementary education, secondary education, and K–9 administration and supervision.

In 1965 Mr. Kamm married Lynne Pazdera. They taught at Summerfield together, and Mrs. Kamm also taught in the Illinois schools of Herrin, Collinsville, and St. Mary's School in Trenton. A well-respected and talented teacher in her own right, Mrs. Kamm taught reading in the Wesclin school district before her retirement.

The Kamms have two sons. Eric is a computer systems architect and vice president with Analytic Innovations in Oak Park, Illinois. Charles Jr., director of choirs at Vassar College for 6 years, is currently in the doctoral program at Yale University.

There are two grandchildren in the family, Noah and Emma, who now share the adventures of Griswald, the kindergarten bear who traveled West with their grandparents many years ago.

Mr. Kamm was a member of the teacher advisory council at McKendree College, and recipient of three awards from his alma mater: Charter Member of the Excellence in Education Honor Society, Distinguished Alumnus Award for Contributions to Teacher Education, and the Career Achievement Award for Exemplary Service in the Field of Public Education.

He was featured as an outstanding educational leader in the *St. Louis Commerce Magazine* for his work in promoting and supporting innovative teaching techniques at Summerfield, and documented as an exemplary teacher and administrator in the text *Teaching Language and Literature in the Elementary Classroom: A Professional Handbook* (Popp, 1996).

Mr. Kamm remains active and involved in the school and community, serving as a driver for Senior Nutrition Meals and for Voluntary Interfaith Caregivers. As a member of this group, Mr. Kamm helps provide transportation for people who need a ride to the doctor, to church, or the grocery store.

Mr. Kamm is an accomplished photographer, and has had his *Photographic Landscapes of the American West* displayed for public viewing in various venues.

REFERENCES

Adams, H. (1999). *The Education of Henry Adams: An Autobiography*. New York: Random House.

Ashton-Warner, S. (1986). *Teacher*. New York: Touchstone.

Banks, L. (1999). *Indian in the Cupboard*. New York: Camelot.

Beck, L. (1994). *Reclaiming Educational Leadership as a Caring Profession*. New York: Teachers College Press.

Blase, J., & Kirby, P. (1999). *Bringing Out the Best in Teachers: What Effective Principals Do* (2nd ed.). Thousand Oaks, CA: Corwin.

Carle, E. (1990). *The Very Quiet Cricket: A Multisensory Book*. New York: Philomel.

Carle, E. (1999). *Rooster's Off to See the World*. New York: Aladdin.

Chion, L. (2001, February 17). Frosty Warms Audience with Warm Praise. Interview in *The Conference Daily*. Arlington, VA: American Association of School Administrators.

Covey, S. (1991). *Principle-Centered Leadership*. New York: Simon & Schuster.

Dewey, J. (1985). *The Middle Works, 1899–1924, Vol. 9*. Carbondale: Southern Illinois University Press.

Dewey, J. (1991) *The Later Works, 1925–1953, Vol. 13*. Carbondale: Southern Illinois University Press.

Dickinson, E. (1957). *Poems by Emily Dickinson*. Boston: Little, Brown & Company.

Duncan, K., & Nickols, D. (1944). *Mentor Graham: The Man Who Taught Lincoln*. Chicago: University of Chicago Press.

Gardner, J. (1961). *Excellence: Can We Be Equal and Excellent Too?* New York: Harper and Row.

Lee, H. (1960). *To Kill a Mockingbird*. New York: Warner Books.

Little, J. (1991). *Listen for the Singing*. New York: HarperCollins.

Loehring, W. (1989). *Where Are You From?* Kansas City, MO: John Bower.

Lyman, L. (2000*). How Do They Know You Care? The Principal's Challenge*. New York: Teachers College Press.

MacLachlan, P. (1987). *Sarah, Plain and Tall*. New York: Harper Trophy.

McPhee, J. (1986). *Rising from the Plains*. New York: Farrar, Straus & Giroux.

Mosel, A. (1989). *Tikki, Tikki, Tembo*. New York: Henry Holt.

Nave, G. (1981, December). He Distinguished Himself. *The Lebanon Advertiser*, p. 1.

National Association of Elementary School Principals (2001). *Leading Learning Communities: Standards for What Principals Should Know and Be Able to Do*. Alexandria, VA: NAESP.

Norris, C., Barnett, B., Basom, M., & Yerkes, D. (2002). *Developing Educational Leaders: A Working Model—The Learning Community in Action*. New York: Teachers College Press.

North, S. (1990). *Rascal*. New York: Scott Foresman.

Pasi, R. (2001). *Higher Expectations: Promoting Social Emotional Learning and Academic Achievement in Your School*. New York: Teachers College Press.

Patterson, J. (1993*). Leadership for Tomorrow's Schools*. Alexandria, VA: Association for Supervision and Curriculum Development.

Phi Delta Kappa Workshop. (1972). *Teacher Appraisal for Instructional Improvement*. Bloomington, IN: Phi Delta Kappa.

Popp, M. (1996). *Teaching Language and Literature in Elementary Classrooms: A Handbook for Professional Development*. Mahwah, NJ: Lawrence Erlbaum.

Schertle, A., & Shute, L. (1987). *Jeremy Bean's St. Patrick's Day*. New York: Lothrop, Lee & Shepard.

Sernak, K. (1998). *School Leadership: Balancing Power with Caring*. New York: Teachers College Press.

Spinelli, J. (2000*). Maniac Magee*. New York: Little, Brown & Company.

Stuart, J. (1958) *The Thread That Runs So True: A Mountain Teacher's Story*. New York: Touchstone.

Webster. D. (2001) *The Great Speeches and Orations of Daniel Webster*. Frederick, MD: Beard Books.

Whitman, W. (1996) *Walt Whitman: Selected Poems*. London: Orion.

ABOUT THE AUTHOR

Marcia S. Popp was an elementary teacher, college professor, and director of teacher education at McKendree College in Illinois. She is also the author of two college-level textbooks and a collection of interviews with retired Olympic athletes.

DATE DUE

MAY 2 2 2009			
MAR 2 5 REC'D			
MAY 1 7 2010			
MAY 1 4 REC'D			
GAYLORD			PRINTED IN U.S.A.